W9-DIT-987

EXPLORING CAREERS IN MIDWIFERY

EXPLORING CAREERS

IN MIDWIFERY

By
JENNIFER CROFT

The Rosen Publishing Group, Inc.
NEW YORK, NY

Published in 1995 by The Rosen Publishing Group, Inc.
29 East 21st Street, New York, NY 10010

First Edition

Library of Congress Cataloging-in-Publication Data

Croft, Jennifer, 1970–
    Careers in midwifery / by Jennifer Croft.
        p.   cm.
    Includes bibliographical references and index.
    Summary: An overview of the history of midwifery, the categories of certification and training, birth settings, career planning, and midwives and the health care debate.
    ISBN 0-8239-1957-9
    1. Midwives—Vocational guidance. [1.Midwives—Vocational guidance. 2. Vocational guidance.] I. Title
RG950.C76 1995
618.2'0233—dc20   95-24603
                                                                        CIP
                                                                        AC

About the Author

Jennifer Croft is an editor and free-lance writer in new York City. A graduate of Columbia University, she became interested in midwifery during a fieldwork study of traditional Indian midwives that she conducted while studying and traveling in northern India in 1992. An article about this study was later published in *Midwifery Today* magazine. Ms. Croft has worked as a volunteer at women's health organizations in the New York Area.

Contents

Introduction   v
1. The History of Midwifery   1
2. Childbirth Issues   13
3. Certified Nurse-Midwives   26
4. Independent Midwives   37
5. Birth Settings   48
6. Serving the Public Through Midwifery   70
7. Opportunities for Adventure   76
8. Midwifery-Related Careers   84
9. Planning Your Future   95
10. Midwives and the Health Care Debate   101

Glossary   103
Appendix   105
For Further Reading   132
Index   135

Introduction

It's an exciting time to enter the field of midwifery. Birth centers are springing up all over the country, each with its own unique philosophy of birth. Midwifery education programs are thriving. More and more hospitals are adding midwives to their staffs. For the general public, the word "midwife" no longer conjures up an image of a hunch-backed old woman with a bag of mysterious herbs: Midwives are increasingly known and accepted as an alternative to the care provided by obstetricians. The title of an *Elle* magazine article in April 1993, "Midwife Crisis: Women Want More," is indicative of the growing demand for midwifery services in this country. And why not? Midwives provide safe, effective, high-quality care at a reasonable cost. For practical reasons alone, midwifery makes a great deal of sense. Beyond that, it represents a different way of looking at birth that appeals to many parents-to-be. The midwife philosophy maintains that birth is a normal, natural process that should proceed without complications if the mother is healthy and not at special risk. The midwife is present at birth to facilitate its normal course, not to change it, speed it up, or utilize forms of intervention (unless absolutely necessary). Midwives also believe in giving the mother and her partner the freedom to make their own decisions about the birth. If the woman wants to sit, stand, eat, drink, or have her other children present at the birth, for example, she is allowed to do so as long as it is safe for both her and the baby.

Midwifery is a time-honored profession that is

practiced in societies all over the world. In the United States today, midwives work in all fifty states in a variety of settings. From large public hospitals in poor urban areas to posh private birth centers to births in clients' own homes, midwives have a degree of flexibility and variety uncommon to other professions. This applies to work hours, too; working nights, working nine-to-five, or working alternate days of the week are all within a midwife's range of possible schedules.

While the number of midwives has doubled in the last ten years, demand still exceeds supply. The American College of Nurse-Midwives predicts that by the year 2000 midwives will deliver 10 percent of all births. In an environment in which many obstetricians and physicians are opting out of the birth business because of astronomical malpractice insurance premiums, the need for accessible, high-quality maternity care is greater than ever.

The national media have taken notice of the trend. Several years ago, the television program *Nightline* noted that "thousands of American women are turning to midwives." On *Today*, it was observed that "as obstetricians drop out of business at the alarming rate of 12 percent a year, midwives are making a comeback." The actress Cybill Shepherd has spoken about her positive experience with a midwife and says that she still has a friendship with the midwife who delivered her baby. "I felt I had control . . . I felt supported," she says. Midwifery has even appeared on best-seller lists in the form of novelist Gay Courter's books about Hannah Sokolow, a midwife on New York's Lower East Side in the 1990s. They have proved to be enormously popular. And don't forget the International Day of the Midwife, May 5 of every year.

Why has the idea of midwifery caught on? Probably because it's an idea that makes a lot of sense. People served by midwives like the idea of having personalized, affordable health care. And for midwives themselves, the career can be both financially and personally rewarding. Remember, however, that the career of midwifery is not for the weak-of-stomach, nor for the person seeking a quiet desk job. It requires enormous amounts of energy, flexibility, compassion, dedication, medical expertise, and interpersonal skills, in addition to many other qualities. If these qualities describe you—and if you have a sincere commitment to improving the health of women and children—then read on. As we approach the twenty-first century, the field of midwifery is changing rapidly and reestablishing its foothold in our society. You can be a part of this fascinating event.

1

The History of Midwifery

She summoned the midwives,
He worked the clay.
She sang the sacred song,
He prayed the special prayer.
She finished singing,
She pulled off fourteen pieces of clay.
She divided them into rows of seven,
She set up the birth stool between the rows.
She summoned the midwives,
She mounted the birth stool.
She counted ten months,
They determined her date.
The tenth month came,
She went into labor.
Her face was beaming,
. . . full of joy.
She put on her cap,
She began to midwife.

This story from an ancient Sumerian myth puts midwives at the forefront of the process of creating life. In the Atrahasis story, the divine midwife is given the assignment of creating humans to do work because the gods have tired of doing everything themselves. The story was also known among Assyrian and Babylonian peoples

Certified nurse-midwife Elinor Buchbinder talks with a couple as she shows them the hospital birthing room. Many hospitals have added birthing suites to attract patients seeking a more homelike environment.

and is said to have parallels with the Mesopotamian epic of Gilgamesh as well. The midwife is a very powerful figure, charged by the gods with the responsibility of introducing human life. This very early reference to midwives makes it clear that they have probably been around as long as life itself.

Considering a career in midwifery is to consider becoming part of an ancient tradition. It is believed that the mother of the philosopher Socrates was a midwife. After all, women have always had babies, and there has always been a need for someone to support and assist a laboring mother and to provide immediate care for a newborn child. Often this role fell to older female relatives, but sometimes certain women in the community became especially skilled at delivering babies and were called to attend births. They were often considered wisewomen, respected for their knowledge about illness and health.

In some traditional societies, midwifery is an occupation practiced within families. In such societies, if your mother or grandmother is a midwife, she may train you as a midwife too. In traditional Indian culture, for example, women of a certain caste are the midwives for their communities.

MIDWIVES IN EUROPE

Midwifery has been called the world's oldest helping profession. But the history of the profession has not been without controversy. In 1484, during the late Middle Ages, two German monks published a treatise called *Malleus Maleficarum* (The Hammer of Witches). All Roman Catholic judges and magistrates in Europe were required to read this text. It described the wickedness of women, witches, and midwives in particular.

> Witch midwives cause the greatest damage, either killing children or sacrilegiously offering them to devils. . . . The greatest injuries to the Faith are done by midwives; and this is made clearer than daylight itself by the confessions of some who were afterwards burned.

The authors recommended that midwives be tortured. They were, and worse; it is believed that thousands, perhaps millions, of midwives were executed in a frenzy that spread from Germany to the rest of Europe and England.

3

Perhaps one of the reasons midwives often suffered stigmatization was that they were the persons in the community who dealt most often with life and death and with what were considered "polluting substances" like blood and childbirth-related fluids. Midwives were caught in a situation where their skills, though highly valued, were at the same time denigrated as being "dirty." The work of the midwives was also suspected to be somehow magical, and it was feared that they had special powers that they could just as easily turn against the community. After all, if a midwife could heal, could she not also inflict pain? A literary example of the persistent bias against midwives appears in *Martin Chuzzlewit* by Charles Dickens. The book features a midwife named Sairy Gamp "whose nose in particular was somewhat red and swollen. . . . She went to a lying-in or a laying-out with equal zest and relish" (lying-in refers to childbirth, and laying-out refers to preparing a body for burial). Here Dickens emphasizes the midwife's connection with both birth and death, painting it in an unfavorable light.

MIDWIFERY IN THE UNITED STATES

In the United States, midwifery has a shorter but equally turbulent history. Midwives were common and generally accepted in colonial America, as they had been in the settlers' home countries in Europe and England. But the fear and distrust of midwives followed the settlers across the Atlantic. When Anne Hutchinson, a midwife in Massachusetts, delivered a baby with a birth defect, she was accused of witchcraft and banished from the state. When she died, the church bells rang for twenty-four hours.

In *A Midwife's Tale*, historian Laurel Thatcher Ulrich pieced together parts of the diary of Martha Ballard, a midwife in Maine who delivered 816 babies between 1785 and 1812. Ulrich illustrates how Ballard and other women like her formed an economic network which, though often ignored by historians, was crucial to the functioning of colonial society. Like her fellow midwives during this period, Martha Ballard worked not only with women in childbirth but with many sick or dying members of the community: children, men, and women. She often used local herbs in her remedies. In other words, in those days a midwife was a healer and caregiver for the entire community, involved in all stages of life, not just childbirth. Many midwives today base their work on this tradition by providing care to women throughout their life cycles, not just in childbirth; it is known today as "well-woman care."

Sometimes in colonial America men attended births when a midwife was not available. They were known as man-midwives or barber-surgeons. Because they lacked the midwife's experience and knowledge of natural methods, the man-midwives often employed more invasive techniques, such as the use of forceps or hooks. The field of obstetrics, designed to give man-midwives more training, was introduced in American medical schools in the eighteenth century. Midwives, on the other hand, were not allowed to receive training in surgery and anatomy. The introduction of anesthesia in the mid-nineteenth century gave doctors an added advantage, as women were understandably anxious to lessen the pain of childbirth.

The medical profession began to gain power and influence in American society in the 1800s. Doctors reasoned that women who came to them during childbirth would come to them for all their other health needs. The first step in inducing women to abandon midwives in favor of doctors was to discredit midwives. To gain more clients for themselves, the new breed of obstetricians sought to paint midwives as old-fashioned, unscientific, and incompetent. The ruse worked, especially in the middle and upper classes of society. The doctors, mainly upper- and middle-class men, simply had more political influence than the midwives did. They managed to convince people that childbirth attended by an obstetrician in a hospital was safer than birth at home with a midwife. Physicians used their influence to have laws banning midwifery passed by state legislatures. In at least one state, Massachusetts, they succeeded. In fact, the United States is the only country in the world where midwifery has ever been outlawed.

Despite the efforts of the medical profession, many American women, especially rural and working-class women, still put their trust in their local midwives. As large numbers of Europeans immigrated to American cities in the 1880s and 1890s, many midwives came along as well. These "Old World" midwives delivered the babies of many working-class immigrant women in urban areas. Because they were recent immigrants, midwives were looked down upon by some as un-American, even though midwives had been here since the arrival of the Mayflower. In 1900, midwives still delivered half of all babies in the United States, and only 5 percent of babies were born in hospitals. (In fact, Jimmy Carter was the first American President to be born in a hospital.)

In 1910, a national survey called the Flexner report studied the growing profession of American medicine. One of its recommendations was that doctors should try to "drive midwives out of the maternity field and promote obstetric physicians, raising obstetrical fees so the field would attract able men." The report stated blatantly that midwives should be eliminated for the economic benefit of doctors. In 1911, an American obstetrician named Dr. J. Whitridge Williams published

6

an article, "The Midwife Problem and Medical Education in the United States," in which he described how the dangers of childbirth pointed to the need for obstetrics as a medical specialty. He, too, recommended the elimination of midwives.

Another concern of doctors was that midwives were caring for poor women, who were seen by some doctors as the raw material with which to gain clinical experience. The perceived need for "guinea pigs" gave doctors another reason to eliminate midwives. Medical schools and charity hospitals, which served large numbers of poor people, developed a relationship whereby medical students could practice their skills on those without the means to afford better care. Because these doctors-in-training were eager—indeed, often were required—to practice the latest techniques (whether or not they were necessary), normal deliveries were often interfered with for the sake of trying out surgical innovations and medications, a practice that probably caused much unnecessary pain and anguish to the mothers involved.

Were doctors justified in their portrayal of midwives as dangerously unskilled practitioners? Studies indicate that midwives in fact often had better medical records than the doctors themselves. To be sure, some midwives probably did practice unsafe methods, but this can be attributed less to the incompetence of midwives as a whole than to the lack of education and supervision they received. In countries such as England and Holland, where midwives were trained and licensed, they were incorporated into the medical establishment rather than kept out of it. Thus they were equally able to benefit from advances in medical knowledge. In New York City, the work of Dr. S. Josephine Baker to regulate and supervise midwives was critical to reducing that city's infant mortality rate by half by the 1920s. She

7

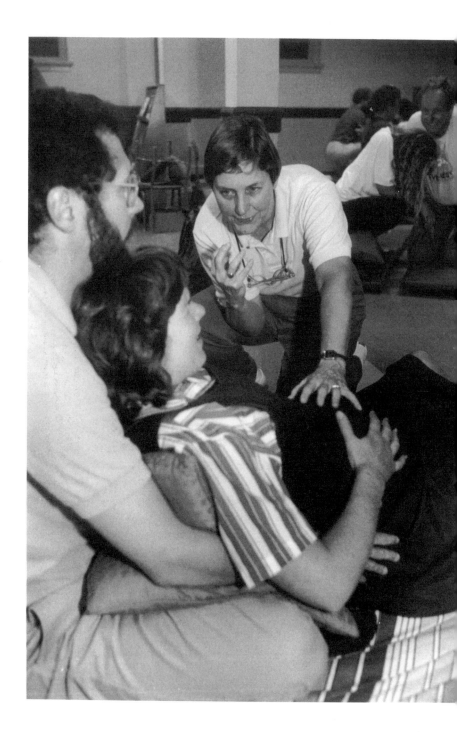

oversaw the establishment of the first city-run school for midwives in the United States, at Bellevue Hospital. In New Jersey, midwives could be licensed as early as 1892, and by 1915 they were required to have a two-year course of instruction. Most of the midwives who took part in New Jersey's programs were recent immigrants from southern and eastern Europe. Beginning in 1927, the state published a magazine called *The Progressive Midwife*, probably the first of its kind. Georgia and other Southern states, where midwives delivered a large percentage of births, adopted regulatory programs.

But even as midwives seemed to be making something of a comeback, at least in the care of poor and rural women, the medical profession became increasingly entrenched in the realm of childbirth. The use of sedation, episiotomy, forceps, and other procedures was becoming routine. The view of childbirth as a healthy, normal process began to change to that of an illness requiring medical attention. In opposition to this trend, in 1933 the English doctor Grantly Dick-Read published *Natural Childbirth*, encouraging education, exercise, and deep breathing to keep women relaxed during labor. Later, the French doctor Fernand Lamaze recommended similar methods. Many hospitals did adopt the recommendations of Dick-Read and Lamaze and began offering classes in natural childbirth or childbirth preparation. At the same time, however, articles by doctors began appearing that criticized the

Penny Simkin, an internationally known childbirth educator, coaches a couple in a childbirth preparation class in Seattle. In many childbirth preparation classes, partners participate and play an important role.

natural childbirth movement, describing it as a step backward.

Evidence of the discontent felt by American women at the impersonal and sometimes even cruel treatment they received at the hands of doctors came in the form of a series of letters to the editor run in the *Ladies' Home Journal* in 1957 and 1958. It all began when a registered nurse who wished to remain anonymous wrote to the magazine describing some of the horrors she had seen in the delivery room. A flood of letters followed from women backing up the nurse's description with their own experiences. Women reported being strapped to the delivery table and left alone for hours, even deprived of the presence of their husbands. They told of having their legs strapped together to prevent their baby from being born before a doctor was available. One woman even testified that a nurse had sat on her knees to keep her legs together until the doctor arrived.

Many nurses responded to the letter as well, corroborating the horror stories and criticizing their fellow members of the medical profession for poor ethical behavior. In 1955, the *Journal* published "Babies Should Be Born at Home" by anthropologist Ashley Montagu. Montagu recommended the revival of midwifery. Despite the dissatisfaction with hospital birth, however, there were few other options for women, and the generally negative response to Montagu's recommendations indicated that women weren't quite ready to consider birth out of the hospital.

The growth of the women's movement in the 1960s and 1970s fueled greater interest in natural childbirth, homebirth, and midwifery, as women sought to free themselves from what many saw as a misogynistic medical establishment. The 1979 book *Our Bodies, Ourselves*, a groundbreading symbol of the women's health movement, advocated the use of midwives for maternity care. Another radical book, *Immaculate Deception* by Suzanne Arms, opened the eyes of many to the state of American birth. Arms compared the situation with those in Holland and Denmark, where obstetricians were not so powerful and where birth results seemed to be better than in America. Although they had separate origins, the natural childbirth movement and the women's health movement, which was an outgrowth of the feminist movement, became increasingly linked in many people's minds.

In many rural communities in California, midwives became a popular alternative for people seeking to return to more "natural" ways of life. In 1971, the famous Birth Center in Santa Cruz, California, came into being at the intiative of midwife Raven Lang. Alternative birth centers emerged in other parts of the country, and in response to patient demand, birth centers and birthing suites were incorporated into many hospital obstetric wards. But the fight to reduce medical intervention in childbirth and to give women greater control over their birth experiences was not yet over; indeed, it continues today.

The Granny-Midwife Tradition

The American South has always had a strong tradition of midwifery in the form of granny-midwives, also known as grand midwives. Granny midwives were African-American women who served as health care providers to their communities. Traditionally, they learned their skills from their mothers or grandmothers who had been midwives before them. During the early 1900s, almost 90 percent of African-American babies in the South were delivered by midwives. As late as the 1960s, hundreds of granny midwives were actively practicing. As people turned for care to modern medical facilities, the granny midwives were no longer the community's main health care providers. In poor and isolated rural areas, however, they continued to be important.

In a March 1994 *Essence* magazine article, midwifery is described as a way for African-American women to keep in touch with their cultural heritage. "In a natural birthing environment, our strong southern, Caribbean, and African birthing traditions are more likely to remain intact," writes Kimberley Knight.

2

Childbirth Issues

It goes without saying that as a midwife you'll have to understand the process of childbirth from the inside out. In fact, you'll have to understand all aspects of a woman's body through all her stages in life. Midwives don't just arrive at a birth and "catch the baby." You must know a patient's history and body extremely well and be able to use that knowledge as your client progresses through her pregnancy. She may seek your care before she is pregnant, too. You may serve clients who are not, have never been, and have no plans to be pregnant: they may be teenagers getting their first menstrual period or women approaching menopause. It's all part of a midwife's job.

As a midwife, you'll be at the frontlines of a battle within the medical community. Childbirth is a controversial subject these days. Medical techniques that were once promoted as safe and effective are increasingly under fire as dangerous to mother, baby, or both. Unfortunately, disagreement on some of these issues pits midwives against doctors, when these two groups should work together and learn from each other. Technology, surgical intervention, and drugs are important issues in childbirth that you should study carefully to decide your own position. Keep in mind that midwives deal with normal, healthy, low-risk women, which forms the basis of their noninvasive approach to childbirth. If you are more interested in the application of technology to high-risk pregnancies, midwifery is probably not right for you. In the midwifery model, the woman giving birth is the heroine, not the caregiver.

Pregnancy

Before learning about the controversial issues in childbirth, it is necessary to know the basics of childbirth itself. What exactly is involved in pregnancy? You've probably learned in school all about conception—that is, how a woman gets pregnant in the first place. What happens after that may be a little less clear.

About seven days after conception, the group of cells that will become the embryo attaches itself to the wall of the uterus. A normal pregnancy can be anywhere from 200 to 300 days in length. The sign of pregnancy that is noticed first by most women is amenorrhea (absence of menstruation). It is at this point that a woman often seeks out a medical practitioner, be it doctor or midwife, to determine whether or not she is pregnant. Or she may seek confirmation of a home pregnancy test that has been positive. Other possible symptoms of pregnancy include morning sickness, frequent urination, swollen breasts, food cravings, or changes in the color of vaginal and cervical tissue. Besides home pregnancy tests, blood or urine tests for pregnancy can be conducted in a lab or an office setting.

Once the embryo is firmly in place, the pregnancy proceeds as follows:

Month 1: The embryo is tiny. During these first few weeks, the neural tube, which will become the brain and spinal cord, begins to form. Also forming at this time are the heart, the digestive tract, and arm and leg buds.

- **Month 2:** The embryo becomes a little longer (although still not much more than an inch long) and has a beating heart. Bone starts to replace cartilage.
- **Month 3:** The fetus is now several inches long. Organs begin to develop, including the reproductive organs. The circulatory and urinary systems are operating.
- **Month 4:** The fetus now has the ability to suck and swallow, in addition to other reflexes. Fingers and toes are well defined, and tooth buds have appeared. The fetus looks more "human."
- **Month 5:** The fetus (now about nine inches long) starts to grow hair, eyebrows, and eyelashes and is covered by a protective coating.
- **Month 6:** If given intensive care, the fetus might survive if born now. The eyes are open, and finger and toe prints can be seen.
- **Month 7:** The fetus is displaying more behaviors, such as crying, thumbsucking, even hiccuping. Fat may be deposited on the body. Stimuli such as light and sound may cause the fetus to respond.
- **Month 8:** At this time, growth proceeds rapidly, especially growth of the brain. The fetus can now see and hear, and other systems are developed.
- **Month 9:** The lungs are fully developed. When born, the average baby weighs about seven and a half pounds and is about 20 inches long.

During pregnancy, women often experience nausea, bloating, constipation, mood swings, back pain, and swelling. A good diet and exercise program, however, can reduce many of the unpleasant aspects of pregnancy.

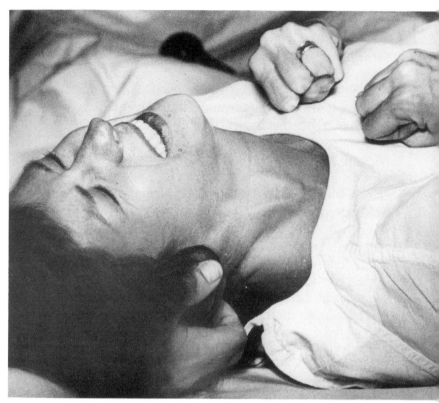

For many midwives, one of their occupation's chief rewards is observing the joyous and exhilarating process of childbirth.

A qualified midwife is knowledgeable about nutrition and fitness and can advise clients on how to best take care of themselves. Of course, pregnancy can still be an uncomfortable and difficult experience for many women. Midwives work with women to lessen any fears they may have and to help them to cope with both the physical and emotional aspects of pregnancy.

Prenatal care is critical to a healthy pregnancy and delivery. Proper prenatal care has been shown to affect pregnancy outcomes dramatically and result in healthier babies. Midwives are skilled providers of prenatal care. At a prenatal visit, a midwife:

- Checks the mother's weight to make sure that the baby is growing normally and to determine whether the mother is gaining excess weight.
- Checks the blood pressure.
- Tests the urine for protein and sugar content (high levels of either may indicate pregnancy-related illnesses such as diabetes or toxemia).
- Measures the abdomen to track the growth rate of the fetus.
- Feels the baby's position and location (important for detecting abnormalities such as a breech position, for example).
- Listens to the baby's heartbeat using either a Doppler ultrasound device or a fetascope (a stethoscope with a special adapter).

LABOR

In the ninth month of pregnancy, a woman's body begins to produce a hormone called oxytocin. Oxytocin causes the uterine muscles to contract and sets off labor. The body prepares itself for the baby: The cervix becomes completely dilated (opened), and the muscles of the uterus work to push the baby down and out. The "breaking of the waters," which is usually the sign that labor has begun, is a signal that the membranes of the amniotic sac have ruptured. The "water" is actually amniotic fluid, in which the baby has been floating for the past nine months.

The nature and length of a woman's labor varies widely from person to person. Some women have their baby in a matter of hours, hardly realizing that they are in labor until the baby is almost ready to come out; other women labor for days. As a midwife, you are with

17

your client throughout the entire process. The support, encouragement, and medical assistance you provide at this time can make a huge difference in a woman's childbirth experience.

Sometimes labor does not progress normally. Some babies just need more time getting out, but a prolonged labor can be a sign of a problem: the baby is too large for the mother's pelvis, or the baby is not in a good position. Even emotional reasons can inhibit the progress of labor. A woman may feel doubts about her ability to cope with the oncoming pain of labor, or she may fear that the baby will emerge flawed in some way. The reassurance and support of a partner, labor coach, or midwife can help a woman deal with emotional obstacles. Dealing with a client's emotional needs will be a large part of your job.

Labor Positions

In movies and TV, when women give birth, it's usually lying flat on their backs in a hospital bed. In fact, this position, known as the lithotomy position, is used so routinely that it is often regarded unquestioningly as the best position in which to give birth. For the doctor, this is probably true: After all, with the woman lying on her back it is most convenient for the doctor to see what is going on. But for the woman herself, and indeed, for her unborn baby, this position is not particularly comfortable or efficient. Because the uterus is pressing on a major blood vessel, blood flow to the baby is decreased. In addition, the mother must work against the force of gravity to push her baby out. The chances that the woman will need an episiotomy are increased.

Squatting, sitting up in bed, lying on one's side, and on one's hands and knees are positions that make more sense. Midwives in hospitals may be restricted as to what positions their clients are allowed to assume, but in general midwives work with a client to determine which position is most comfortable for her. Birthing stools and birthing chairs are used by some midwives.

Natural Childbirth

The idea of "natural childbirth" became popular in the 1970s as people became disillusioned by the medical treatment of childbirth and sought more "natural" alternatives. Basically, natural childbirth refers to unmedicated, family-centered childbirth where the mother's own decisions are respected. Natural childbirth aims to counter the idea of medicalized childbirth, in which birth becomes a medical event treated as an illness. Today, midwives generally agree that a "natural childbirth" should in theory be drug-free, but they emphasize that women who feel they need medication should not feel that they have not had a natural childbirth. The most important principle is that women should feel in control of their own birth experience.

THE POLITICS OF CHILDBIRTH

Why use invasive procedures when they are not needed? Part of the reason is economic: Hospitals can charge more for high-tech births than for low-tech ones. In addition, the use of invasive techniques may be seen by some hospitals as a way to minimize the potential for complications. If a patient is dissatisfied with the outcome of a birth, the hospital wants to be able to show that the doctor did everything technically possible to ensure a good outcome (even though it is sometimes technology itself that interferes with a good outcome). Obstetricians pay the highest malpractice insurance rates of all medical specialists. This is partly a reflection of the fact that they face high-stakes malpractice suits more often than other physicians.

As a midwife, it will be important for you to have a

solid understanding of childbirth technology and its applications. Although you will not make use of this technology, since your specialty will be low-risk births, your very decision to become a midwife is a decision not to participate in a high-technology framework, and thus is a somewhat political one. Midwives and doctors approach obstetrical technology differently because they approach birth differently in general. The midwife model of birth is quite distinct from the medical model. As noted by Patricia Burkhardt, Coordinator of the Midwifery Program in the Division of the Nursing at the School of Education at New York University: "Physicians are educated in a disease-focused model. OB/GYN is a surgical specialty. The mindset of physicians is disease-focused, and this impacts clearly on their care. This is how past practices developed: Every woman had a shave, an enema, an IV. A midwife would only do that if it were helpful. There are no routine procedures. To a midwife, reproduction is a normal process. Her job is to enhance and facilitate that mother's ability to do it well. A midwife is a knowledgeable, skillful observer of the process."

The following are some controversial topics in childbirth. Even within the midwifery community, opinions vary on these issues. No matter what your stance on certain procedures, you may be required to perform them in certain settings, such as in a hospital having strict procedural protocols.

Episiotomy

An episiotomy is a surgical cut of the vaginal opening designed to make more room for the baby to come out and to prevent tearing of perineal tissues. While the idea makes sense, the problem is that many episiotomies are made unnecessarily and cause the mother unnecessary pain during and after the birth. In cases of breech birth or fetal distress, however, or if there is a risk that without an episiotomy the woman would suffer serious lacerations, the technique can be useful. This was the conclusion of a study of more than 1,000 births conducted in Montreal in 1992. The study found that episiotomy "may be of no medical benefit, and may make recovery more difficult" and is needed "only in cases of distress to the baby." Midwives generally try to avoid performing episiotomy, but for many doctors it is a routine practice, a habit that is difficult to break. It is performed in most first births at hospitals and in about half of all subsequent births. Episiotomy is often justified on the ground that without it the woman will tear anyway; but midwives employ techniques that lessen the risk of tearing in the first place, such as allowing the woman to deliver in a squatting position or massaging her perineum. Because episiotomy is considered so routine by so many doctors, they are often not knowledgeable about techniques that may eliminate the need.

Drugs

Drugs may be administered to the mother to induce labor or relieve pain. But are drugs always needed? In general, midwives use a minimum of drugs or use them only when a mother requests a pain reliever. Some are quite skilled at the use of herbal remedies.

Analgesics are drugs that decrease the perception of pain, and anesthesia removes the sensation of pain. Epidural anesthesia, which is common in many hospitals, is administered through a catheter placed in the woman's back, near the base of the spinal cord. Epidural anesthesia numbs the area between the abdomen and the knees. A major drawback to epidural anesthesia is that its use is often accompanied by other procedures such as an IV attachment, vacuum extractor or forceps delivery, and

21

the administration of other drugs. A common analgesic used during birth in hospitals is Demerol, which is most effective when injected intravenously. Its side effects may include nausea, vomiting, depression, and lowered blood pressure; the drug may also slow down contractions and make the woman drowsy. While some women greatly appreciate the pain relief, others dislike the feeling of not being in control that may accompany Demerol.

Around 1914, an anesthetic called "Twilight Sleep" was introduced and grew rapidly in popularity. It was a mixture of morphine and a hallucinogenic and amnesiac called scopalomine. The effect on laboring mothers was that although they experienced the pain of childbirth, they remembered none of it afterward. What many women did remember, however, was having been in a disoriented, nightmarish state, a memory that haunted them later. In *The American Way of Birth*, Jessica Mitford reports that Twilight Sleep may still have been in use as late as the 1970s in some hospitals.

Pitocin, a labor-inducing drug in use today, has been the subject of controversy. Pitocin is a synthetic form of the hormone oxytocin. It causes extremely intense contractions of the uterus that can be very painful for the mother, in addition to making her feel as if she has lost control of the labor. Pitocin also has the potential to cause hyperstimulation of the uterus and bring on fetal distress.

Doctors have been accused of using Pitocin to speed up labor for their own convenience. For midwives, who prefer to let labor take its natural course, this is not an issue. In fact, many believe that a labor may be "slow" only because of a woman's immobility and the fact that she is forced to lie on her back, the position most convenient for the doctor. The midwife philosophy is that women should be able to move around during labor and give birth in whatever position they choose, regardless of how long it takes. Many midwives believe that invasive procedures such as the electronic fetal monitor (discussed later) actually slow down the labor process, which is then used as an excuse to use drugs, creating a vicious circle.

Cesarean Section

In a cesarean section, or C-section, a surgeon makes an incision slightly below the pubic hairline and removes the infant from the mother's uterus. (The cesarean section is so named because it is believed that Julius Caesar was born this way.) In some cases a cesarean section is necessary, but it is often performed simply to avoid possible complications of a vaginal birth. Many midwives believe that this is not a sufficient reason to perform the operation and argue that it poses other risks for the mother, as well as increasing the likelihood that her future births will also have to be cesarean. Although it was formerly believed that a woman could never have a vaginal birth after a cesarean ("Once a cesarean, always a cesarean," it was said), a growing number of women have achieved this successfully. It is known as VBAC (pronounced veeback).

For the birthing mother, a cesarean can be a painful, drawn-out procedure. She usually needs more painkillers than a mother who has delivered vaginally, and it takes her longer to recover, resulting in both a longer hospital stay and a longer recovery time out of the hospital. The risk of infection increases after a C-section, and antibiotic treatment can affect breast milk. The mortality rate for cesarean mothers is higher than the rate for mothers delivered vaginally. Clearly a cesarean section is not something to be taken lightly. In certain cases, of course, it is a lifesaving procedure; but too often the need for a cesarean is overdiagnosed because of

23

physicians' fear of being held liable if something goes wrong in a vaginal birth. A report by the Institute of Medicine in 1989 stated, "There is overwhelming evidence that part of the recent rise in the cesarean section rate in this country is the result of the medical-legal environment."

A midwife would never perform a cesarean section, as it is a major surgical procedure. She might determine that it was necessary in an emergency situation and would then arrange for the patient to be transferred to a doctor. However, there is evidence that midwifery care throughout a pregnancy significantly reduces the chances that a woman will need a cesarean section. Midwifery care has been credited with maintaining very low C-section rates in European countries; in the Netherlands, for example, the national rate is 8.5 percent compared to a rate of 25 percent in the United States.

Electronic Fetal Monitoring

The practice of electronic fetal monitoring became especially common in hospitals in the early 1970s. The electronic fetal monitor, or EFM, is a device that is attached to the mother's abdomen to record the baby's heart rate and to detect abnormalities and fetal distress. An internal fetal monitor consists of electrodes connected to wires that are attached by metal clips or screws to the baby's head. The problem? For the EFM to work, the mother must lie immobile, which is often uncomfortable for her and can inhibit the process of labor. In addition, there is a tendency for hospital personnel to become dependent on the EFM and act too hastily in the belief that complications have developed. The EFM has been linked to an increase in cesarean deliveries, for instance. Studies have proved no significant advantage of the EFM over listening to a baby's heartbeat with a stethoscope, and the device has the added disadvantage of focusing everyone's attention on the EFM rather than the patient. High cost is another drawback: Used routinely during childbirth, the price comes out to $750 million a year. Eliminating its routine use could save up to $675 million a year.

3

Certified Nurse-Midwives

As the title indicates, a certified nurse-midwife (CNM) is both a certified nurse and a midwife, having had training in both fields. Certified nurse-midwives currently number around 4,500 in the United States and its territories, and the number is growing. Like midwives in general, their duties include client screening, prenatal care, labor and delivery, postpartum care, family planning counseling, and gynecological care throughout a woman's life. In about half of all states, nurse-midwives have the authority to prescribe drugs.

About 4 percent of all births in the U.S. are delivered by nurse-midwives. Of these births, almost all take place in hospitals (94 percent), with 3.8 percent occurring at birth centers and 2.3 percent at home.

Certified nurse-midwives work in private, public, or military hospitals; birthing centers; health maintenance organizations; public health departments; private practices; and clinics. Some nurse-midwives also attend homebirths or run their own home birth practices. Nurse-midwives work in a team approach with doctors, nurses, and other specialists. As a nurse-midwife, you have many options to choose from. Here are a few:

- Working in a private practice staffed entirely by midwives

- Working in private practice with a physician
- Combining work in a birth center with a home-birth practice.

THE HISTORY OF NURSE-MIDWIFERY

In 1917, the maternal and infant mortality rate in the United States was the highest of any developed country in the world. The profession of nurse-midwifery in the United States developed as the result of a recognized need for improved maternal-child health care. In the early 1900s, the Children's Bureau in Washington, DC, recommended that public health nurses provide prenatal instruction in an effort to combat appallingly high infant and maternal mortality rates. The first prenatal care pilot project in New York City in 1918 found that prenatal care significantly reduced maternal and infant mortality. In this same period, the Maternity Center Association in New York City began to look overseas for solutions to the problem and found that the countries with the most impressive maternal-child health statistics were those where nurse-midwives figured prominently in the maternity cycle. The Association began to operate its own childbirth education classes and prenatal clinics.

Meanwhile, a Kentuckian named Mary Breckinridge, who had received her training as a nurse-midwife in England, knew firsthand of the important role played by nurse-midwives in maternal care. In 1925, she brought nurse-midwives from Great Britain to provide much-needed health services to isolated rural communities in the Appalachian mountains. The success of the program was convincing. (The Frontier Nursing Service tradition continues in the Frontier Graduate School of Midwifery, still in operation.)

In 1931, the Maternity Center Association established the nation's first school of nurse-midwifery. In an important step toward legitimizing the status of the nurse-

27

midwife, the American College of Nurse-Midwifery was formed in 1955; in 1969, it merged with the American Association of Nurse-Midwives and changed the name to the American College of Nurse-Midwives. Today the ACNM is the professional organization for certified nurse-midwives in the United States. New Mexico, in 1945, became the first state to licensed nurse-midwives. In 1959, a similar law was passed in New York City. In 1958, Kings County Hospital in New York began the first nurse-midwifery program at a major hospital with a university affiliation. The United States Air Force was the first military service to employ midwives and started its own school of midwifery in 1973. The U.S. Army and Navy also use midwives to deliver the babies of servicemen and women.

In 1971, a milestone was reached in midwifery history when the American College of Obstetricians and Gynecologists and the American College of Nurse-Midwives issued a joint statement that "qualified nurse-midwives may assume responsibility for the complete care and management of uncomplicated maternity patients." Midwives had finally been endorsed as legitimate providers of maternity care. The 1970s and 1980s were a time of increasing popularity and acceptance for CNMs. The number of practicing CNMs shot up from 275 in 1963 to 1,712 in 1976 to 2,550 in 1982.

A Growing Need for Nurse-Midwives

Currently, there are about 300 new nurse-midwives every year, but the number does not seem to be enough. The American College of Nurse-Midwives has set a goal of 10,000 CNMs by the year 2001. Between 1975 and 1988 there was a 500 percent increase in hospital deliveries by nurse-midwives. Many hospitals are increasing their nurse-midwifery staffs. In fact, at

Katsi Cook, left, a Mohawk midwife, talks with a woman at the Akwesasne Mohawk Indian Reservation.

some hospitals an incoming patient may never see a doctor—the pregnancy and birth are handled by a midwife from start to finish. Caring for birth in this way is less expensive for both the hospital and the patient, and many patients appreciate having continuity of care by one nurse-midwife throughout pregnancy. Patricia Burkhardt stresses the growth and change in the field of midwifery. "If you project this career over twenty years, there is a void to be filled," she says. "A person entering the field will have lots of opportunities."

Many professional sources and medical experts have recognized the importance of nurse-midwives in maternal and child health and have described the

numerous benefits of nurse-midwifery services. Nurs
midwives have been credited with increasing access
prenatal care, thereby helping to prevent low bir
weight babies, premature births, stillbirths, and cesare
sections. The Institute of Medicine reported in 19
"Certified nurse-midwives . . . have been shown to
particularly effective in managing the care of pregr
women who are at high risk of low birthweight because
of social and economic factors. These health care
providers tend to relate to their patients in a non-author-
itarian manner and to emphasize education, support,
and patient satisfaction. For example, several studies
have shown that women served by nurse-midwives are
more likely to keep appointments for prenatal care and
to follow specified treatment regimens."

A 1994 study conducted by researchers at the Albert
Einstein College of Medicine in New York City found
that babies born to mothers who had been under the
care of nurse-midwives were just as healthy as babies
whose mothers had been treated by obstetricians.
Further, they found that the mothers who had received
nurse-midwifery care rated themselves as more satisfied
with the birth experience than their counterparts who
had been treated by a physician. Cassandra Henderson,
a doctor who worked on the study, commented: "This
suggests that using nurse-midwives is an option that
should be available to all women."

A Day in the Life of a Certified Nurse-Midwife

When asked to describe a "typical day" at work, many
midwives are quick to point out that there's almost no
such thing. Simply working in a medical environment
seems to guarantee a certain degree of unpredictability.
Still, there are hospital routines that one should expect
to follow. Lauren Abrams, a certified nurse-midwife in
New York, works three days a week at a hospital and

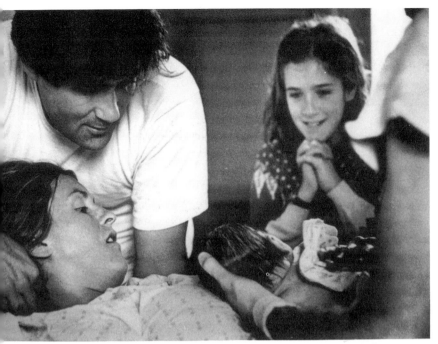

Midwives often encourage family members to be present at births.

one day at a clinic. When she is working at the hospital, she arrives at about 7:30 a.m. She puts on scrubs and goes to the postpartum floor, where mothers who have just given birth are recuperating. Abrams describes postpartum care as the midwives' top priority. There, she checks the women's labwork for any problems. She then examines the patients and answers any questions they may have, counseling them on family planning, nutrition, breast-feeding, and how to take care of themselves. If they are ready to go home, she prepares the paperwork for discharging them from the hospital.

Next, she goes to the labor and delivery floor. She looks into every room and examines everyone's chart. If a patient has an uncomplicated course of labor, she is a candidate for a midwife, at which point Abrams would take over for the resident on duty. After reading the patient's chart, she would give any needed medication. In the delivery room, usually (though not always) a nurse and a support person (the baby's father, for example) are also present. If there are any problems, Abrams consults with a physician. Even if she has to turn the delivery over to a doctor, however, she still stays with the patient. Her day usually ends around 7 p.m. Her days at the clinic involve more counseling, prenatal care, and treatment of other health problems.

At Abrams's hospital, midwives work day shifts; any night deliveries are handled by residents. The physicians and residents at the hospital are very appreciative and supportive of the midwives' work, she says, as are the patients.

Certified Nurse-Midwifery Versus Independent Midwifery

The legal status of midwifery in the United States varies widely from state to state and is changing rapidly. One thing is certain: Certified nurse-midwives have fared better than independent midwives in achieving the right to practice legally in every state. If you plan to stay for many years in a state where independent midwifery can be legally practiced, you may not find it necessary to consider certification as a nurse-midwife. If you think that you may want to live in more than one state, only as a certified nurse-midwife can you be guaranteed that you will be able to practice legally wherever you go. However, midwifery advocacy organizations are working to establish nationwide guidelines for the certification of direct-entry midwives.

In most states, certified nurse-midwives also have the advantage of being able to receive reimbursement from many private insurance carriers, Medicaid, Medicare, and CHAMPUS (Civilian Health and Medical Program of the Uniformed Services). However, a new law in Oregon makes it possible for independent midwives to be reimbursed through Medicaid if they pass state licensing requirements, and other states are considering similar legislation.

Some midwives find that practicing nurse-midwifery in a hospital offers the best of both worlds in that the highest degree of technology is available in case of emergency, but women also have the option of having relatively technology-free births. Working in a hospital also provides job stability, regular hours, a steady salary, and benefits. The downside, according to some midwives, is that midwives in hospitals have less freedom to make decisions because they must follow hospital policies with which they may not always agree. Says one nurse-midwife, "It is a constant struggle with the interns to cut fewer episiotomies and give the women fluids to drink."

STUDYING TO BE A CERTIFIED NURSE-MIDWIFE

To practice as a certified nurse-midwife, you must complete a program of certification that is accredited by the American College of Nurse-Midwives. The ACNM also administers the national certification exam for nurse-midwives. As of 1993, there were 35 accredited nurse-midwifery programs. These programs are competitive; to be accepted it is important to succeed in your high school and college studies.

First of all, you must be a licensed registered nurse (RN) before becoming a nurse-midwife. Becoming an RN involves either graduation from a four-year university program with a baccalaureate degree (BSN) in nursing, or graduation from a two-year college program with an associate degree in nursing (ADN). Some nurse-midwifery programs, however, offer a three-year plan in which the student studies nursing during the first year and earns a master's degree over the next two years. Programs of this type require that you already have a bachelor's degree. Yale University, Columbia University, and the University of California–San Francisco are among the schools offering programs of this type. Midwives who studied other subjects in college often find that this broadens their experience in a positive way.

Hands-on experience in maternity care or a clinically related area is required for eligibility for most nurse-midwifery programs. For some programs, such as the University of California–San Francisco, knowledge of Spanish and experience working with underserved populations is encouraged. For master's programs, applicants are generally required to take the GRE (Graduate Record Examination). Some programs have other requirements such as the completion of an introductory statistics course.

Nurse-midwifery programs are of three types. A **basic certificate program** provides all the essential components of a nurse-midwifery curriculum. This course of study takes about nine to fourteen months. Nurses with a two-year associate degree or diploma are eligible for this kind of program. A **basic graduate program** provides all the components of the basic certificate program but is incorporated into a program of professional studies leading to a master's degree. This requires about sixteen to twenty-four months of study. For some programs, the GRE may be required. A **precertification program** provides only selected components of the nurse-midwifery curriculum. It is for registered nurses who are already recognized professional midwives in a foreign country, or for nurse-midwives already certified in the U.S. who are preparing to reenter clinical practice.

The student who has completed one of these three programs may sit for the national certification board examination administered by the American College of Nurse Midwives, which is offered in various U.S. cities every month. Once you have passed the examination, you can be licensed to practice in any state. (The appendix lists accredited nurse-midwifery education programs in the United States.)

What will you learn in a nurse-midwifery program? According to the American College of Nurse-Midwives, the subjects are the following:

- Primary and gynecological care (physical examinations, screening and diagnostic tests such as Pap smears, contraception, making diagnoses, and identifying health problems)
- Preconception and prenatal care (counseling women about nutrition and other health habits that can affect a pregnancy, prescribing medications and treatments, conducting screening tests for a healthy pregnancy)
- Labor and delivery management (providing physical and emotional support to mothers in labor, repairing lacerations and episiotomies, and administering anesthesia)
- Postpartum and infant care (counseling mothers in breast-feeding and care of newborn, assessing health of infant, managing discomforts after childbirth).

Nurse-midwifery programs provide a combination of academic training and clinical experience.

The American College of Nurse-Midwifery has also developed a community-based training program for nurses who want to become midwives. Similar to some direct-entry education programs, the Community-based Nurse-Midwifery Education Program (CNEP) allows nurses to do coursework at home and to complete their clinical work with a local nurse-midwife practicing in a hospital or birth center.

Funding for Study

Many sources of funding are available to the nurse-midwifery student, including Division of Health Services scholarships, the loan repayment program of the Indian Health Service, American College of Nurse-Midwives scholarships, and scholarships offered by many individual organizations and agencies. The financial aid officer at the school you are considering attending will be able to help you find the assistance you need. Another possible option is to persuade a local hospital, clinic, or private practice to sponsor you in return for a commitment to work for them after you graduate. The higher education and public health departments in your state may also have funds for study.

Salaries

Starting salaries for nurse-midwives are generally very good, in the range of $40,000 to $60,000 a year. According to the American College of Nurse-Midwives, the average income of nurse midwives in 1993 was $55,000. One large cost for nurse-midwives is malpractice insurance, which can be as expensive as $13,000 a year. Naturally, a nurse-midwife employed by a hospital or a physician in private practice will have a steadier income than one who is self-employed, but some nurse-midwives enjoy the greater flexibility and independence of working on their own, and some private practices can be quite successful financially.

4

Independent Midwives

Independent midwives are also known as direct-entry, traditional, community, or lay midwives (although "lay midwife" is a somewhat controversial term.) The term direct-entry refers to the fact that independent midwives do not become registered nurses before becoming midwives. Instead, they are educated through a combination of academic study, apprenticeship, and hands-on experience. State licensure and certification of independent midwives has been adopted by some states as a way to regulate their activities. While licensure is seen by some midwives as beneficial because it enables them to practice without fear of legal action, others believe that it entails an excessive degree of state control over their occupation. State-certified midwives must usually take the North American Registry of Midwives (NARM) exam.

INDEPENDENT MIDWIVES AND THE LAW

Before setting out to be an independent midwife, you must determine the status of midwifery laws in your area. Decisions about the practice of midwifery are handled by state health boards or state legislatures. In Illinois, Indiana, Iowa, Kentucky, Maryland, Missouri, North Carolina, Ohio, Virginia, and West Virginia it is illegal for direct-entry midwives to practice at all, although campaigns are currently being waged to change the legislation in all of these states. In other states, midwifery is simply "alegal": The law does not address it. This is the case in Alabama, Connecticut, Idaho, Kansas, Nebraska, South Dakota, Vermont, and Wisconsin (although legislation is pending in Nebraska and Kansas).

States in which midwifery is legal by licensure, registration, or certification include Alaska, Arizona, Arkansas, California, Colorado, Delaware, Florida, Louisiana, Minnesota, Missouri, Montana, New Hampshire, New Mexico, New York, Oregon, Rhode Island, South Carolina, Texas, and Washington. In Georgia, Hawaii, and New Jersey, midwifery is legal but a license or permit is not yet available. In Maine, Massachusetts, Michigan, Nevada, North Dakota, Oklahoma, Pennsylvania, Tennessee, Utah, and Wyoming, midwifery is legal through judicial interpretation but not regulated by the state.

Medicaid, the government health insurance program for low-income and unemployed Americans, has been extended to cover the expenses of direct-entry midwifery care in Alaska, Oregon, Washington, Florida, and New Mexico. For direct-entry midwives, this is an important step toward achieving recognition and legitimacy; it also offers the potential to serve many more clients. The new law makes economic sense for the state, too, since the costs reimbursed to midwives will be lower than the costs for doctors. Medicaid already reimburses the cost of care by certified nurse-midwives in all states.

Eliminating the nursing requirement for midwives has been suggested as a way to deal with the current shortage of midwives, but it is unlikely that such a change will occur nationwide anytime soon. The Midwifery Communication and Accountability Project (MCAP), a Massachusetts-based organization, is seeking the recognition of all certified or licensed midwives (both direct entry and CNMs) at the state and national levels. MCAP has facilitated and encouraged collaboration between the American College of Nurse-Midwives and the Midwives' Alliance of North America (a national organization representing direct-entry midwives). Direct-entry and certified nurse-midwives have often been seen as separate, distinct groups in the past and have even seemed at times to be at odds with each other. Today, however, they seem to be finding common ground and working together to make midwifery available to all women.

BECOMING AN INDEPENDENT MIDWIFE

An independent midwife might start out by simply being present at homebirths and assisting with child care, cleanup, or food preparation. Accompanying a woman to the hospital as a labor support person is another way to get exposure to the birth process. You might ask your local hospital if you can volunteer as a labor coach.

To gain the experience you need, it is crucial to find a midwife who will let you be an apprentice. If you do not know of a midwife, your state midwifery association might be able to refer you to practitioners in your area. You and the midwife must determine whether you are compatible to work together for as long as a year or more. For you, it is important to have the opportunity not only to watch and learn but also to be able to ask questions and even offer your own insight when appropriate. The senior midwife should be someone with whom you are comfortable and enjoy working.

In the beginning of your apprenticeship, you might just watch the midwife at work, perhaps providing her with supplies as needed. The next step might be to learn how to take fetal heart rates, check blood pressure,

39

Julia Lange sits with a former client and the daughter Lange delivered. Lange and other independent midwives in many states have had to fight for the right to practice midwifery.

perform vaginal exams, and even repair vaginal tears. Gradually you will have more opportunities to try out what you have learned, perhaps culminating in a delivery with you in charge from start to finish and your senior midwife observing.

The Midwives' Alliance of North America (MANA) has developed a set of guidelines to help aspiring midwives choose a midwife to apprentice with. MANA suggests that when interviewing a midwife who is willing to take you on as an apprentice, you consider the following:

- What are her qualifications? How many deliveries has she attended? (It is best to apprentice with a midwife who has attended more than 100 deliveries.) What kind of education did she have? Is she licensed or certified? Can she show you her statistics regarding neonatal deaths, maternal problems, or hospital transport? Does she work well with other midwives and health care workers in the community?

• How large is her practice? Is it large enough for you to gain significant experience?

• Can both you and the midwife define your expectations for the apprenticeship? Can you reach a financial agreement?

• Has she had an apprentice before? (If so, it is a good idea to talk to that person.) What does she feel are her strengths and weaknesses in teaching midwifery?

• Will the midwife provide you with adequate hands-on experience? How will she evaluate you? Will you have proper supervision?

DIRECT-ENTRY MIDWIFERY EDUCATION

Theoretical study is also a component of a direct-entry midwifery program. This study can be either formal or informal. A formal program might mean that you register at a school and attend classes there. A formal school can offer the advantage of providing the possibility of state licensure or certification. The accessibility of faculty is also a definite advantage. An informal program may be self-designed, perhaps even a home correspondence course. If you want to set up your own course of study, speak with other midwives and with your state midwifery association for advice on what courses will be useful. You might take anatomy or biology courses from your local university or community college, for example. In any case, it is important to cover all your bases and establish a program of study that is affordable, feasible, and complete. A self-designed program of study will require you to be highly self-disciplined and motivated.

A home study course can provide you with a pre-designed curriculum having greater flexibility than classroom study. If you live in an area without a formal midwifery program nearby, a home study course may be your only option unless you are willing to relocate for a period of time. The Apprentice Academics Midwifery Home Study Course is designed to take about three years to complete. Students submit assignments as they complete them, and an annual report is due once each year.

In Arizona, where direct-entry midwives can qualify for state licensure, the Northern Arizona Institute of Midwifery offers a program of professional education. Students receive a theoretical education, but they do not actually attend classes in a particular setting. Courses are designed to blend with clinical activities so that students receive a balance of coursework and hands-on experience. The curriculum is divided into three phases, with five or six module courses in each phase. The student completes the modules, which include courses in maternal-infant nutrition, genetics, communication and counseling skills, and pharmacology, on a self-study basis. Selected projects from each module are requested by the Institute and evaluated by an education committee of midwives. An approved preceptor, who can be a midwife or a physician, oversees the student as she or he completes a total of 1,000 hours in a clinical setting, in addition to attending 50 births. Every year, an evaluator from the Institute makes a visit to the student's preceptor site to evaluate progress. The prerequisite for the program is the completion of 27 college credits: 3 credits each in English, psychology, nutrition, human growth and development, and sociology or anthropology, 8 in human anatomy and physiology, and 4 in microbiology. (There is some flexibility in the requirements, however.) In addition to a $100 application fee, the student pays $750 per module and covers the cost of the evaluator site visit.

There are also schools at which you can receive certification as a midwife. If there is such a school near you, or if you feel that you function better in a classroom setting, this may be the route for you. The Seattle Midwifery School is an example of a program in which courses are taught in classrooms, and clinical courses are completed in a variety of settings in the U.S. and abroad. The program is generally completed in three years. The school also offers an extension education program, with courses on labor support, women's health and nutrition, and neonatal resuscitation.

A unique training program is offered by Maternidad La Luz, a combined birth center and midwifery program in El Paso, Texas, a city that has been called the heart of midwifery in the United States. The center, staffed by regular staff and students, has a mostly Spanish-speaking clientele and cares for approximately fifty women every month. The programs offered include a complete six-month academic and clinical program; a three-month introductory course; and a three-month advanced course (for students already trained as health care providers.) Students who complete the six-month program are eligible for internships at the birth center. Students work 24-hour shifts three times weekly, becoming involved in the full scope of midwifery care as they conduct prenatal appointments and work with patients in labor while fitting in classes on nutrition, emergency situations, and newborn adaptation, among many other subjects. One day a week, class time is devoted to "birth talks," when the births that occurred during the week are reviewed and discussed.

The Midwives' Alliance of North America has developed direct-entry core curriculum guidelines that you should know as you plan your course of study. The curriculum is divided into the areas of basic sciences, social sciences, health sciences, professional studies, health education, and midwifery. Basic sciences includes such topics as embryology, genetics, and pathophysiology. Social sciences encompasses psychology and the study of women, families, and societies. Health sciences includes human sexuality, epidemiology, and physical assessment.

GAINING EXPERIENCE

Most midwifery programs prefer for applicants to have several years of experience in the labor-delivery field. And most midwives agree that hands-on experience is absolutely essential to becoming a good midwife. Rebecca Wrigley of Portland, Oregon, is working at a local birth center before going on to midwifery school. She already has her nursing degree, but it may be five to seven years, she says, before she goes to a midwifery program. "The degree of responsibility involved in midwifery seems to deter people from going directly into a midwifery program," she says, adding that it takes a lot of practice and observation to gain the confidence a midwife needs to do her job well. One of the things that appeals to her about midwifery, Wrigley says, is that there are so many different ways to get experience. She assists with births at the center and helps out with administrative tasks such as hiring new nurses and designing educational curricula. She also visits high schools to talk to pregnant teenagers and give them information about the birth center. Many pregnant teens assume that they must give birth in a hospital, she says, but they should know their other options. "I have an affinity for working with teens," she says. "It's one of my strengths."

Wrigley's interest in midwifery, and in teen mothers in particular, began when she did an independent study project while in nursing school. The project involved working with a team of midwives with pregnant teenagers in an inner city. "The midwives had a different philosophy about teen pregnancy," she says. "Obstetricians generally assume that all teen mothers are high-risk. These midwives did a lot of research and found that for the majority of teen mothers the only risk is that they are not educated about their own needs during pregnancy. The clinic I worked at was run completely by women. It did lots of childbirth education and teen parenting classes." Wrigley says that even as a small child she showed an interest in pregnant women, and as she grew up she wanted to be involved with taking care of babies. "It's an interest I've always had," she says.

In addition to her work at the birth center, Wrigley is starting a new job as a labor-delivery nurse. She is trying to get experience in as many birth settings as possible. Her goal is to enter a nurse-midwifery program that would allow her to work with both in-hospital and out-of-hospital births. She would also like to combine being a CNM and a Family Nurse Practitioner, to fully realize the idea of a midwife as a primary care provider. Wrigley's career plan is an excellent example of the flexibility midwives have in choosing the sort of population with which they would like to work as well as the setting they prefer. Experiential learning has been critical to Wrigley's decisions about what path her career will take.

Salaries

As one independent midwife says: "It's hard to make a living as a lay midwife." If personal time constraints prevent you from maintaining a very large and busy practice, and you deliver only a few births a month, you may find it hard to make ends meet. If, on the other hand, you are willing to make a large time commitment, you can make a decent living. Independent midwives generally charge a lump sum for all their services, including prenatal care, labor and delivery, and post-partum care; for each birth, this fee may vary from $500 to over a thousand dollars. (Fees vary in different parts of the country.) Many midwives establish a sliding scale, charging the full amount to those who can afford it and offering their services for a lower price, or free, to clients with tighter budgets. Bartering—exchanging services for a client's goods or services—is also practiced by some midwives. For example, a client may have little cash, but perhaps she has a used car she's looking to sell and you happen to need a car. You might work out something whereby she "pays" you by giving you the car.

Because their workloads and the fees they charge vary so much, it is difficult to estimate the average income of an independent midwife. Start-up costs are a factor as well: You have to make an investment in equipment and supplies for your own practice. Going into practice with a partner can help to alleviate high overhead costs.

Making Choices

Whether you decide to become a CNM or a direct-entry midwife depends on many factors. You may simply have an inclination one way or the other. Or perhaps you already have some medical education or training that points you in the direction of nurse-midwifery. On the other hand, maybe the progressive licensing and insurance reimbursement policies in your state provide incentive for you to become a direct-entry midwife. It is a decision you need to make on your own. Talking with different kinds of midwives can be helpful in making a choice. There are, of course, advantages as well as drawbacks to any decision you make. A nurse-midwifery education would probably be more expensive and take longer than certification as an independent midwife, but it might give you more professional flexibility and a higher salary in the long run. As a direct-entry midwife, you would probably have more entrepreneurial freedom; you'd be able to be your own boss. But you might not be able to practice midwifery wherever you go, and you would have to cope with fluctuations in salary and other frustrations of being self-employed.

The length of time you want to spend being trained as a midwife may be an important consideration for you. If you have not yet started nursing school, becoming a CNM can take six to eight years. Becoming a direct-entry midwife may take three years or less. Since you might have to relocate to complete your studies, think about how long you can be away from home, or whether you'd like to relocate completely.

You must also evaluate the quality of the educational route you choose: Are the teachers experienced and qualified? Will you have access to libraries, computers, and qualified experts? Will you have to relocate to find a quality educational program? Are you ready to make that commitment?

Once you have decided which route you will take, you have another choice to make: what kind of birth setting you'd like to work in. This is discussed in Chapter 4.

5

Birth Settings

Now that alternatives in birth are becoming more common, it is easy to forget that thirty years ago there was no question about where to give birth (in the hospital, of course!), whereas a hundred years ago it was taken for granted that birth would occur at home. Today, for increasing numbers of women, the choice is no longer automatic. In many parts of the country, options are proliferating: birth centers, hospital birthing rooms, homebirths, even waterbirths! Where someone decides to give birth is an extremely personal choice. As a midwife, you also have a choice to make about the kind of birth setting in which you would like to work. A good way to get a feeling for this is to talk to midwives who work in various settings. Ask them what they like and dislike about their work environments. Also visit a variety of birth settings to see where you feel most at home. Take some time to think about what would be your own choice of birth settings if you or your partner were to give birth. What would be your ideal site for the birth process? Your own home? A traditional hospital room? What, in your opinion, is the most pleasant place to give birth?

Each kind of birth setting, of course, brings with it a different style of work for the midwife and a whole new set of factors for you to think about. Ask yourself these kinds of questions:

- Do I like to work as part of a t
  own?
- Can I work a very flexible schedul
  regular hours?
- Can I deal with fluctuations in in
  need a regular paycheck?
- Do I want to be my own boss, or would I prefer
  to be part of a staff?

HOMEBIRTH

Sandra was enjoying a normal, healthy pregnancy, and she and her husband Gene decided that there was no reason why she could not give birth to their baby at their home, an old New England house where Gene's grandfather had also been born. Their midwife, Heather, agreed that they were ideally suited to a homebirth. Just to be sure, Gene and Sandra paid a visit to Dr. Carmichael, who was Heather's backup obstetrician at the local hospital. Dr. Carmichael agreed that Gene and Sandra should not have any problems.

Sandra went into labor on a snowy November night. She called Heather and told her how she was feeling; Heather advised her to take a warm shower, walk around the house, and eat if she was hungry. Even though she didn't expect Sandra to enter active labor for hours, Heather decided to give herself some extra time in the inclement weather. She called her assistant, Monica, and advised her to do the same. Packing a snow shovel in the back of her car, she set out for Gene and Sandra's house. When she arrived, they were dancing slowly in the living room to a favorite album. Sandra's sister, who lived nearby, was in the kitchen making tea and coffee for everyone. Heather complimented Gene and Sandra for being so relaxed and for following her suggestion and preparing a small suitcase just in case a hospital transfer was needed.

49

everyone chatted, listened to music, and sipped coffee while encouraging Sandra, whose contractions were slowly intensifying.

One of your options as a midwife is to practice homebirth—that is, attend women who have decided to stay at home to give birth. Traditionally, babies were always delivered at home, and in many countries they still are. In Holland, for example, half of all births occur at home with a midwife in attendance. Homebirth is virtually a necessity in remote or undeveloped parts of the world, where hospitals are not readily accessible.

Some people believe that home is the best place for babies to be born. Among the reasons they cite are that the mother may be more relaxed in a familiar environment, there is less chance of undesired medical intervention being imposed on the mother, and family and friends can be invited to take part in the experience. Homebirth is also much less expensive than birth in a hospital.

Homebirth began to be considered a real option in the 1970s, when interest in natural childbirth blossomed. It is still fairly rare in this country. Only about 4 percent of all births attended by nurse-midwives occur at home. Of all births, planned births at home probably comprise about 2 to 3 percent of the total.

Is Homebirth Safe?

Homebirth is not without controversy. Even though midwives accept only low-risk patients as clients, many people believe that any birth outside of a hospital is dangerous. What if complications arise and the mother must be rushed to the hospital? Is the home environment sufficiently sterile? Of course, there is always a risk of something going wrong, but childbirth by nature carries a risk. Midwives try to reduce the chances of misfortune

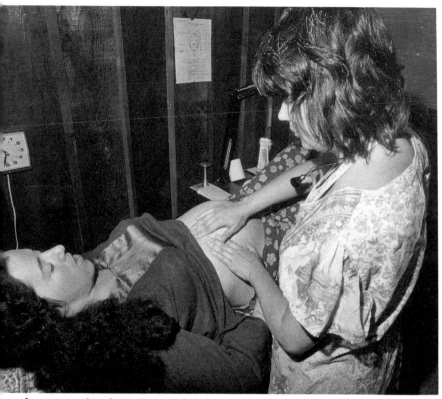

A woman planning a home birth is examined by her midwife.

by selecting only low-risk women as clients, by providing proper prenatal care and education, and by insuring that they have all the equipment they need, including sterilized instruments and sterile gloves. Midwives also have a medical backup for any delivery; if complications do occur, the midwife can call an obstetrician for help.

The International Childbirth Education Association supports homebirth with the following provisions: a certified midwife or physician in attendance; back-up care; prenatal care; screening for high-risk women; a prior home visit; adequate supplies and transportation; and a newborn exam and follow-up. The qualified midwife always follows these guidelines.

Despite the persistent doubts about homebirth, studies show it to be quite safe. A six-year study by the Texas Department of Health in the 1980s, for example, demonstrated that homebirths had a lower infant mortality rate than hospital births. It has been suggested that the risk of infection is lessened by giving birth at home because the woman's body is used to the bacteria in her home environment, whereas the hospital, with its many germs and illnesses, may actually be more dangerous.

The Frontier Nursing Service

A shining example of the safety of homebirth, and indeed, of midwives in general, is the Kentucky Frontier Nursing Service, started by the English midwife Mary Breckinridge in 1925. Breckinridge brought other nurse-midwives over from England to work among the impoverished residents of Kentucky's mountain communities. Although the women involved in these homebirths were poorly nourished, the Frontier Nursing Service maintained an excellent standard of care. The mortality rate for both women and their babies proved to be lower than in the rest of the United States during the same period. In fact, in twenty-three years of service the Frontier Nursing Service midwives were responsible for no maternal deaths.

Homebirth Legislation

Before you make the decision to practice homebirth, inquire of your state board of health or board of midwifery about the laws in your state. In some states, it is illegal for anyone except doctors to deliver at home. In New Mexico, however, an independent midwife may not only perform homebirths for low-risk women but may also receive reimbursement from health insurance policies. Many midwives have found themselves under legal pressure to stop performing homebirths. To avoid that situation, check out the conditions under which you may practice homebirth in your state.

The legal risks of performing homebirths became all too evident for two midwives in Santa Cruz, California, in 1974, when a pregnant investigator for the California Department of Consumer Affairs went undercover to solicit their services and had them arrested for practicing medicine without a license.

Generally, but not always, midwives who perform homebirths are independent midwives: that is, midwives trained through study, apprenticeship, and hands-on experience. Sometimes they are licensed or certified, sometimes not. Practicing homebirth without a license is not recommended for anyone; you might find yourself in legal trouble. State health regulations are designed to protect the public. When a consumer seeks out a licensed or certified midwife, she should know what that midwife's qualifications are. Obtaining the necessary certification protects both you and your clients.

Certified nurse-midwives may also establish homebirth practices in some states. Currently, about 7 percent of certified nurse-midwives nationwide attend at least some homebirths. You may decide, as a CNM, that you don't want to work in a hospital environment. Of course, that has drawbacks, such as not having paid benefits or a guaranteed salary. Finding medical backup as a homebirth midwife may also be difficult. But if you feel especially drawn to the concept of homebirth, this option may be for you.

Homebirth and Certified Nurse-Midwives

Sandra Fields is a certified nurse-midwife with a homebirth practice in New York City. She has an office where she works two and a half days a week, meeting with clients. In addition, she is on call twenty-four hours a day. In her twenty-year practice, she has been known to deliver as many as ten births a month, but now she generally delivers about three births a month. While acknowledging that her irregular schedule can be demanding, Fields says that for her the tradeoff is worth it. She believes that homebirth has many advantages over birth in a hospital environment; she particularly enjoys the flexibility it gives her as a midwife.

"In a homebirth setting, the midwife is able to individualize management based on knowledge of the client, knowledge of alternative medicine," she explains, adding that there is generally less flexibility in a hospital setting, where the institution is held liable for a midwife's actions. The midwife, while not having to protect an institution, is freer to practice "the art of midwifery," while hospitals promote "the science of midwifery," Fields maintains.

Fields acknowledges that many people consider homebirth unsafe and even harmful. This, she believes, stems from a fear of birth that is promoted by professional medicine. "If there is no fear of birth, there is no fear of homebirth," she says.

Miriam Schwarzchild has had her own homebirth practice in New York for about five years. "I love what I do,"she says. But, she points out, "It's not a good job for people who don't like to be up at night." She adds with a laugh that babies seem to prefer to be born at night. Part of Schwarzchild's original decision to become a midwife stemmed from her perception that midwifery was a very accessible career.

"I wanted to work with a diverse population of healthy women of childbearing age. I knew that midwifery incorporated direct patient care, a lot of teaching, and a lot of political work," Schwarzchild explains. She adds that midwifery can be a very political career if one chooses to focus on that aspect. Her own activism has been in the area of reproductive rights and women's choice. She says that people often have a strong reaction when she tells them that she is a midwife. "Just announcing what you do brings up a lot of feelings and discussion," she says.

The teaching aspect of her job comes into play when she counsels her clients about issues ranging from nutrition to self-confidence, Schwarzchild says. "Pregnancy is a time of stress and emotional growth," she notes. "Women are very ready to absorb information."

Schwarzchild says the idea of homebirth "just seemed to make sense to me. It's connected to choice. I believe that women should have all options available to them. At the same time, many people are angry that homebirth is an option."

After working as a Registered Nurse for two and a half years, Schwarzchild worked on a hospital staff serving low-income women. She also worked on a clinic service and started a private practice at the same time. She did some homebirths on the side before striking out on her own. "The work itself is incredibly flexible as to where and when you work," Schwarzchild says, using her own experience to illustrate that midwifery can encompass a number of settings and schedules. In addition to her current practice, she still works at a hospital one night a week "to keep myself sharp." Her practice is quite busy. She delivers about six babies a month, and has about fifty clients at any given time. She allots three days a week to seeing clients and has two to three births in a typical week. Then she might have a week without any deliveries.

Starting a private practice was not as cost-intensive as one might think, Schwarzchild says. She has a very low overhead, since she sees clients in their own homes. Starting out, a homebirth midwife needs instruments, a backup physician, and mechanisms for charting and keeping track of patient records. Probably the biggest challenge is simply attracting clients, which is not a problem for Schwarzchild at all. Her practice is extremely lucrative, she says, and all her clients are referred to her by word of mouth. But, she points out, the situation might be different in an area with many homebirth midwives competing for clients. Still, she perceives a definite need for more homebirth midwives. "There need to be more midwives doing homebirths so women will know it is an option," she concludes.

Independent Midwives and Homebirth

Julia Lange is an apprentice-taught midwife who has been practicing for twelve years. She is bringing a lawsuit against her state to bring about a change in midwifery legislation, which currently prohibits homebirths for independent midwives. Lange makes it clear that homebirth is not for everyone—only the most low-risk women—but she firmly believes that an independent midwife is fully qualified to deliver babies at home.

Despite legal problems, Lange couldn't be happier with her career choice. She decided to begin delivering babies at home after the birth of her own child. Previously, she had worked as a medical assistant. She worked with one midwife for one year, with another midwife for another year, in a clinic for a year and a half, and as a childbirth educator. In her current practice, Lange delivers five to ten births a month. "There is a night-and-day difference between home and hospital birth," Lange says. "So much bonding happens at homebirth. I encourage fathers to handle their own children. The best feeling is when the birth is over and everyone is snuggled in their own bed. Gentle surroundings make my job easier."

Although making a living from homebirth can be

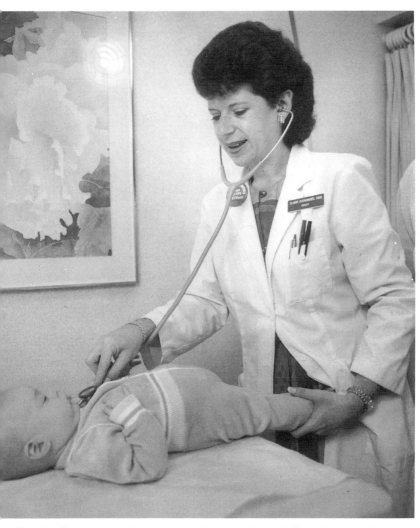

A midwife may continue to provide care to an infant for months after birth.

difficult, Lange says that she has managed as a single mother for seven years with midwifery as her only occupation. She sometimes engages in bartering with clients, and occasionally makes exceptions, such as not charging single parents. "The hours can be very strange and very long," Lange says. "With a homebirth practice especially, you have to give up everything else—one year, for example, I missed each of my kids' birthday parties because I was attending births."

ALTERNATIVE BIRTH CENTERS

Reesa was driving to work one morning when she noticed a new building. It looked more like a house, actually, with a porch and a neat yard where a sign read "Cloverleaf Birth Center." Reesa was intrigued. For her first birth, Reesa had gone to the local hospital. She and her husband Oliver were sure that they wanted to add to their family, but they both wanted this birth experience to be unique. She called the birth center and arranged for the two of them to go for an initial visit with one of the midwives. From the moment they walked in, Reesa and Oliver knew they had come to a special place. "It just didn't have that hospital smell," Reesa says. "There were plants and paintings. The skylights made it seem bright and airy, and the rugs and soft couches in the waiting room made it really cozy." They were greeted by Diana, one of the five midwives on the birth center staff.

"We are all certified nurse-midwives," Diana explained. "I've been practicing for over ten years. I worked in a private physician's practice and then decided that I wanted to start a midwifery practice with some other nurse-midwives I knew. There's a great interest in this community in birth centers. People are ready to try the concept. Like you," she said, smiling, "people are coming here who aren't even pregnant yet!" Diana showed Reesa and Oliver around the facility. They both commented on how clean and well equipped it was, and Reesa especially liked the idea of

having a children's playroom where her son Theo could play if he chose not to watch the entire birth. She also liked the kitchen facilities, where Oliver would be able to fix her favorite meal after the birth was over. She and Oliver thanked Diana and assured her that they would be back in touch to set up an appointment as soon as they suspected that Reesa was pregnant again.

Alternative birth centers are called "alternative" because they offer a nonhospital environment for birth. Also known as freestanding birth centers, they number more than 300 in the United States today. Many pregnant women feel more comfortable in the birth center's more intimate and casual environment. At the same time, birth centers offer a high standard of maternity care. *A New England Journal of Medicine* study gave them a ringing endorsement in 1989: "Birth centers offer a safe and acceptable alternative to hospital confinement for selected pregnant women . . . Few innovations in health service promise lower cost, greater availability, and a high degree of satisfaction with a comparable degree of safety."

A birth center may be decorated to look more like a bedroom or living room than a medical facility, but it is fully equipped to deal with most emergency situations. If serious problems arise, the birth center has a contingency plan to transfer the mother to a hospital. Like midwives in general, birth centers accept only low-risk women who are not likely to experience complications. They provide screening of clients, prenatal care, and postpartum care along with labor and delivery.

Birth centers have become a popular option for many prospective parents. Many women attest that they get more personal care in a birth center than in a hospital; they feel that this personal touch is crucial to a good birth experience. Birth centers offer the additional advantage of being less expensive than hospital births—about half the cost, in fact, and that cost can usually be reimbursed by insurance policies. Family members are welcome at most birthing centers and often have use of kitchen facilities. Birth center staffs encourage mothers and newborns to be back at home soon after the birth, generally within about twelve hours. And many parents enjoy the opportunity to meet other parents in a birth center context.

Birth centers are generally run according to a team approach. This team usually comprises nurses, certified nurse-midwives, obstetricians, pediatricians, childbirth educators, even nutritionists and social workers. Midwives administer the birth centers in most cases but have backup by obstetricians. Birth centers must be licensed by individual states, and many are accredited by the National Association of Childbearing Centers, which in 1983 became the first incorporated organization of birth centers.

In 1975, the Maternity Center Association in New York City opened the first childbearing center in the United States. It has become a model for similar centers around the world. Of course, pioneering is nothing new to the Maternity Center: It was also the site of the first school of nurse-midwifery in America, established in 1931. Gail Sinquefield, a nurse-midwife at the center, is also something of a pioneer. Thirteen years ago, she was the first midwife in New York City to be granted hospital privileges as a nonhospital employee.

In addition to the desk, chair, and bookshelf in her office, there is also a bed where Sinquefield can sleep when she is on call for twenty-four hours. She describes the Childbearing Center as an alternative to home or hospital births, with positive elements of both settings. "For me, the real advantage is that you have a controlled environment where you can set up a system that works. In the hospital, it was frustrating because after delivery I left and my patients were taken care of by the nursing staff, and they didn't always have the same philosophy that I did. The hospital also had some rules that we didn't agree with."

Sinquefield explains some of the features that make the Childbearing Center different from most hospitals. The Childbearing Center does not have a nursery; after the babies are born, they never leave their parents. Family members can stay after the birth for as long as they like, and there is a big bed where everyone can sleep after the delivery. No one is ever "kicked out." "It's an extremely pleasant place to give birth," Sinquefield notes. She says that the comment she hears most often from clients is "It's so quiet!"

The midwives at the Childbearing Center stress that patients should be well informed about their own care and should make their own decisions. Everyone who comes to the Center takes childbirth classes; there are even classes for siblings who plan to be present at the birth of a new brother or sister. "We stress in the orientation [which all prospective patients must attend] that people should look into other alternatives and make an informed decision. We don't put any kind of pressure on people to come here," Sinquefield says. Upon deciding to give birth at the Childbearing Center, a pregnant woman then becomes active in her own care. When patients arrive for prenatal checkups, they examine their own medical records, weigh themselves, and check their own urine sample.

The Childbearing Center approach is noninterventionist; as Sinquefield puts it, "We're very low-tech." That does not mean, however, that the Center is not fully prepared with emergency equipment, and all midwives are trained in neonatal resuscitation. Three

61

physicians are on the staff on a part-time basis. Most patients see a physician once or twice but then see midwives for all other visits. Because the Childbearing Center is a group practice, patients are encouraged to meet all the midwives.

Working at a Birth Center

What is it like to work at a birth center? Sinquefield says that she enjoys the small size of the practice and the chance to get to know people. She describes her work schedule as very workable and humane, pointing out that this is not necessarily common in the field of midwifery. In a two-week period, she works three twenty-four-hour shifts and one twelve-hour day, in addition to keeping office hours one day a week. "We don't have midwives who are tired all the time," she says. "That's a problem in midwifery. But it's ironic because the schedule is also the part that makes it so exciting."

The high stress level of her job is a drawback, Sinquefield says. She emphasizes that the birth center is probably not the right setting for a new graduate; it is important to have enough experience and confidence to make decisions such as whether or not patients should go to the doctor. "If there is an emergency, you must handle it," Sinquefield points out. Although the center has obstetricians on the staff on a consultant basis, midwives attend all of the births. A prospective birth-center midwife would also need to feel comfortable with the technological limitations of the center.

Lynn Whitney, another midwife at the Childbearing Center, had a few minutes to talk after what she called a "borderline labor" where at certain moments she wondered whether the patient would have to go to the hospital. (The mother eventually gave birth in a squatting position.) Whitney says that being on call was

Holland is remarkable for the prominent role midwives play in the health care system. Here, a Dutch midwife discusses the baby's position in the womb with an expectant mother.

hard to get used to. But she describes her job as "really rewarding. It's magical—it's a wonderful feeling helping people to become empowered and to know and trust their own bodies." Whitney says that she always wanted to work in a birth center. "It brought together a lot of things for me—women's issues, counseling, health care."

Sometimes a birth center is owned by a hospital or clinic, relieving the midwives of billing and administrative work. This is the case with Nurse Midwifery Birthing Services (NMBS) in Eugene, Oregon, which was started by two nurse-midwives. Both NMBS and the Childbearing Center follow strict protocols, which is important for several reasons. For one thing, if a client must at some point be transported to the hospital, the birth center midwives must be able to prove that they did everything possible to ensure a successful outcome and to show what procedures were followed. Following protocols also helps the midwives work with each other in caring for patients. Because having a practice with several midwives means that a client will see more than one midwife during her pregnancy, the midwives must be able to take over for each other at any time, and that means knowing what procedures have already been followed with each client. Strict standards ensure that the clients receive consistent care.

The typical patient who comes to NMBS is seeking a balance between midwifery care and easy hospital access. For the midwives, too, it is beneficial to have access to the medical community, which they might not have if they were doing homebirths. NMBS charges clients $2,150 per birth: $1,350 for prenatal care and $800 for the birth center fee. Some clients come to the birth center because their insurance policies do not cover homebirth. In 1992, NMBS midwives delivered 282 births, 73 percent of them with no pain medication.

WORKING IN PRIVATE PRACTICE

"I guess I wanted the best of both worlds," says Sara, a single mother who just gave birth to a healthy boy. She had already been going to Nurse-Midwifery Services for her yearly gynecological exam for years when she became pregnant. "I knew all the midwives; even if they had never treated me, they were always friendly when I came for an appointment. I used to come here for my Pap smear, breast exam, STD screening, and birth control prescription. I liked the fact that all the midwives were women, and they took more time with me than most doctors seemed to. When I wanted to become pregnant, I talked with one of the midwives, Claudia, and she was very helpful. The

support I got here made it a lot easier to consider becoming a single mother."

Throughout her pregnancy, Sara came to the midwives for prenatal exams, and she called the midwife-on-call several times with questions. "Maybe I'm a hypochondriac," she laughs. "But better safe than sorry." When she went into labor, Sara once again called the midwife-on-call, who happened to be Claudia!

"I was happy it worked out that way," Sara says. "But of course I would have loved to have any of the midwives attending my birth. Claudia met me at the hospital, along with a few friends I wanted to be there. We went to the birthing suite of the hospital, which I had already visited, so it looked familiar. I don't really like hospitals, but I feel safer there. Claudia made it feel really comfortable. It was great to have the continuity of care of having my midwife attend my birth while still being in the secure atmosphere of the hospital."

Working in an autonomous midwifery practice may be a happy medium for you if you like the idea of seeing patients in an intimate environment but feel more comfortable having the actual birth take place in a hospital. Fourteen percent of nurse-midwives work in this way. Childbirth Services, or CBS, is an autonomous midwifery practice in New York City. Patients come to the office for consultations, prenatal visits, and well-woman gynecological care; births are delivered at a local hospital where the CBS midwives are on staff. When a patient is in labor, she calls the midwife on call, who provides advice and suggestions until active labor commences; at that point, the midwife meets the patient at the hospital. The midwives try to balance out a patient's twelve to fourteen prenatal visits among them so that a patient never delivers with a midwife she has never seen before (as sometimes happens with doctor-attended hospital births).

CBS is run by three certified nurse-midwives. Barbara Sellars, one of the three, says that after having worked in a variety of situations, she enjoys the autonomy she has at CBS. "I absolutely adore what I'm doing," she says "Every couple is different. Because midwifery is an art as well as a science, it is exciting to be able to use my experience to try to figure things out (for example, why a labor is going or not) and to integrate what I know about the person." A childbirth educator before she became a midwife, Sellars had been frustrated talking with couples who felt they had no say about what went on in the hospital. At CBS, every effort is made to accommodate patients' wishes as long as they do not pose health risks. The care a woman receives at CBS is exactly the same as the care provided by a doctor, Sellars says, except that at CBS an extra twenty to twenty-five minutes per visit are spent with each patient discussing topics of concern such as breast-feeding or circumcision. The patient load is small to prevent burnout among the midwives. In fact, at any one time the majority of patients are not pregnant; they may have delivered already and come back for gynecological care, or they may come simply for well-woman gynecological care.

The downside of private practice, Sellars says, is that one must be aware of the business side of things. Starting any business is a huge risk and can be very stressful and difficult. If you think you'd like to start your own practice, wait until you have a solid reputation in your community. Try to find business partners. You will have to think about finding a space for your business, advertising, getting hospital privileges, hiring employees, and finding a backup physician, among many other things. This may be a goal to work toward many years down the road.

One way that independent midwives often decide to work is in partnership with another midwife. Carla Viles, a midwife in Eugene, Oregon, entered into a partnership with one of the midwives who taught at the private midwifery school she had attended. This worked out well for Viles as a new midwife, since the more experienced midwife already had all the necessary equipment and saved her a large start-up cost. Viles recommends that new midwives starting a private homebirth practice work on building a reputation in the medical community in their area, since this will make it easier to establish back-up support if complications develop. Second, you need to build a reputation in your community so that your clientele will be attracted by word of mouth. Be aware that building a clientele can be slow going at first, but providing quality care and personal attention for each client pays off in the end. Talk to friends and acquaintances about referring their friends and acquaintances to you. You might also consider placing a classified ad in your local newspaper or in a specialized publication pertaining to health or directed at parents or women.

Another private-practice option is working with a physician in his or her OB/GYN practice. This can be a good option if you feel you would enjoy working in private practice but would rather not deal with the business aspect.

HOSPITALS

Wendy didn't really have a choice about where she would have her baby. She is on Medicaid, and in her town only the hospital accepts Medicaid. "I was afraid that my care would be totally anonymous," Wendy says. "I guess I was expecting to be treated like a

67

number, because of horror stories I'd heard. But at my hospital, nurse-midwives deliver all Medicaid patients who are low-risk, and some non-Medicaid patients too.

At first, I didn't even know what a midwife was. I just knew that they were really great to me. I felt that they cared a lot, even though they saw so many patients every day. I guess the best thing was that they stayed with me through my whole birth. I felt like taking a shower at one point early in my labor, and they said that was OK. It's hard to explain, but their support made a huge difference. I'm actually looking forward to going back for checkups. And they gave me great advice about breast-feeding."

The majority of births in the United States, including midwife-attended births, occur in hospitals. The convenience of hospitals is certainly a factor: Not every community has a birth center, and women might not always know how to go about finding a midwife. Sometimes family pressure can influence a mother's choice. Not completely convinced of the safety of birth in a birth center or at home, many women opt for midwifery care in a hospital setting where medical technology is close at hand. You, as a midwife, may also feel more secure in a hospital, especially early in your career. You might regard this as a disadvantage, however: The *Journal of Nurse-Midwifery* reported in 1992 that midwives were more likely to perform hospital procedures in a hospital than in a birth center, and if you hope to use a minimum of invasive procedures you may find it difficult to deal with the pressure to do so in a hospital setting.

Another consideration to working in a hospital is whether you prefer working on a staff or on your own. At a hospital, you won't have the freedom to decide how things will be done all the time. The hospital will probably have strict policies and guidelines that you may at times find restrictive. At the same time, the role of nurse-midwives on hospital staffs is gaining respect, and we might expect that, as a result, midwives will gain more autonomy. For example, while midwives generally work only with low-risk patients, sometimes they can comanage a high-risk pregnancy with a physician.

The regular hours, benefits, and good salaries of hospital-employed nurse-midwives are attractive to many, especially new graduates. It certainly helps that there are many jobs available. Many midwives work in hospitals for a few years and then move on; others enjoy the stability of hospital employment. Volunteering in the birth wing of a hospital as a labor support person can be a good opportunity to see what hospital birth is like.

6

Serving the Public Through Midwifery

Midwifery is by nature a career of service to others. But to a greater degree than many other professions, midwifery offers wonderful opportunities for helping the disadvantaged. Especially in the United States, which has an infant mortality rate above that of many other industrialized nations, and where many people still do not receive the health care they deserve (even though we have the most sophisticated technology available), maternal-child health is an area where extra help is sorely needed. For example, 25 percent of American women receive little or no prenatal care. And all countries of the world where midwives are the principal birth attendants have lower infant mortality rates than the United States.

An important choice you will face is whether to work in the public or private sector. Public hospitals, especially in big cities, often serve poor and minority neighborhoods, and midwives are in high demand. Working in such an environment, you would be dealing face-to-face with such issues as teen pregnancy, drug abuse, inadequate nutrition, and often language and cultural barriers as well. For many low-income women who do not see a health care provider unless they have a gynecological problem, midwives become their primary

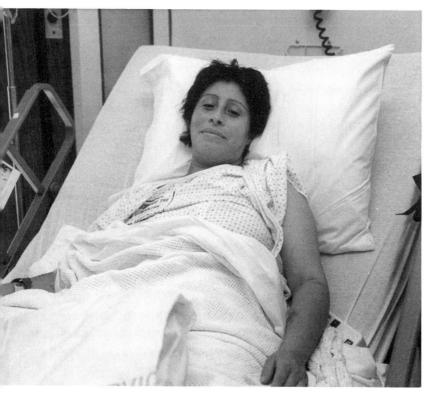

Providing emotional support, as well as medical care, to a woman in labor is part of a midwife's job.

health care providers. Knowing a second language, such as Spanish, can be very helpful when working in an urban public hospital environment. In fact, there are even language courses offering "Spanish for Midwives."

At one large public hospital in New York City, midwives deliver the babies of most incoming patients, many of whom are on Medicaid or have no insurance at all. Midwives are less expensive for the hospital to hire than doctors, and they provide an excellent level of care. A certified nurse-midwife at this hospital describes both the difficulties and rewards of her working environment.

"It's not an ideal place to work," she says. "You are expected to see vast numbers of patients in a short space of time. About 80 percent of patients are from different cultures. Most midwives are obstetrically bilingual, but that doesn't mean that they are culturally bilingual. Some people are clearly abusing the system. Many people have a minimal amount of education; many are high school dropouts.

"There is a high burnout when you get that kind of heavy patient load. It's like a conveyor belt. You'd have to be Mother Teresa to work here for a long time and not be frustrated."

Despite her frustration, this nurse-midwife finds her job rewarding. "It's a wonderful opportunity to help young women take one step forward to being independent, functioning women in society." She manages to find "small miracles" among the many problems she faces every day. For those who enjoy working with people, have an interest in women's health, and do not want a nine-to-five desk job, she says, "it's a great job."

As many public hospitals are striving to increase midwifery services because these services are cost-effective and popular with patients, there is great demand for certified nurse-midwives in hospitals.

The Childbearing Center of Morris Heights in New York City is a shining example of a successful birth center in an underserved neighborhood. Women go through labor and delivery without anesthesia, and a minimum of medical equipment is used. Families are welcome to provide labor support and even cut the umbilical cord. (One patient even invited her church gospel choir to sing in the waiting room while she was in labor.) In a neighborhood that formerly had one of the highest infant mortality rates in the city, the Morris Heights center is making inroads by proving that proper

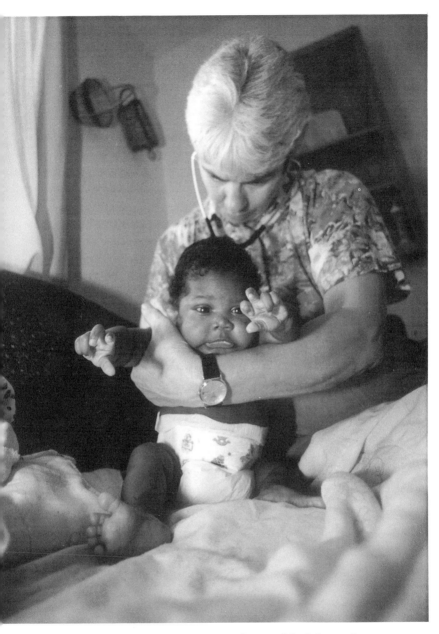

A midwife often provides new mothers with information on breast-feeding and nutrition for their new babies.

prenatal care and education don't have to be expensive to go a long way toward making healthier babies and mothers. With a cheerful atmosphere and bold African prints on the walls, the Morris Heights Center makes women feel welcome. It has become a gathering place for support groups for single mothers, breast-feeding mothers, teenage mothers.

The Indian Health Service (IHS)

Because of lack of economic opportunities, discrimination, and geographic isolation, Native American communities are often underserved in health care. To address this problem, an interesting opportunity for public service is offered by the Department of Health and Human Services of the U.S. government. The Indian Health Service began in 1954, and in 1975 Native American tribes were given the option of managing IHS programs in their own communities. Currently, the IHS operates 364 health care facilities, including hospitals, health centers, school health centers, and village clinics. These facilities are located all over the country but are concentrated in areas such as Oklahoma, South Dakota, and Alaska. The total population served by the IHS numbers over one million.

The Indian Health Service describes as its goal "to elevate the health status of American Indians and Alaska Natives to the highest level possible." Nurse-midwives play an important part in achieving this goal; in 1989, for example, obstetric deliveries and pregnancy complications were the leading cause of hospitalization in IHS areas, pointing to the need for high-quality midwifery services.

To qualify for the IHS, applicants must be U.S. citizens, under the age of 44, and must have graduated from an accredited degree program. Most positions are in rural areas. The IHS offers loan repayment to qualified applicants in exchange for a two-year commitment. If you have an interest in Native American culture, enjoy a rural lifestyle, and would like to contribute your much-needed skill and expertise, the IHS may be worth looking into.

IHS Recruitment Program
Parklawn Building
5600 Fishers Lane
Rockville, MD 20857
(800) 962-2817

The National Health Service

The National Health Service offers scholarships for midwifery students on condition that when the students graduate they will work in places that are underserved in the area of obstetrical care. Lauren Abrams, a certified nurse-midwife at Queens Hospital Center in New York, had her tuition at the Yale Midwifery Program paid by a New York State Health Service Scholarship in exchange for working eighteen months at an underserved location after graduation.

National Health Service Corps
U.S. Public Health Service
1-800-221-9393

7

Opportunities for Adventure

Midwifery may not seem like a career with opportunities for travel, but the midwife who wants to share his or her knowledge and learn from others overseas has many opportunities to do so. Once you have established a practice in your home country, you may decide to see what midwifery is like elsewhere. You can gain valuable perspective on how birth is handled in other cultures. It can be a chance to share your skills with people in need of help. Or perhaps you'd simply like to see a new place or try living overseas for a while.

Your help is very much needed. Every year, the World Bank reports, about 400,000 women die from the direct complications of pregnancy and childbirth. In developing countries, maternal death rates are 30 times higher than in developed countries. In Africa and South Asia, pregnancy-related complications are the leading cause of death among women of reproductive age. In some African countries, obstetricians and gynecologists have abandoned rural areas for large cities. Women giving birth in developing countries may be at higher risk for complications during pregnancy because of factors like poor nutrition, anemia, multiple pregnancies, or being very young or very old. The focus of international health groups is both to eliminate these risk factors and to provide quality care for these potentially high-risk pregnancies.

The training of nurse-midwives has been adopted by many developing countries as a way to solve the problem of high maternal and infant mortality rates. Traditional birth attendants in rural communities have also been targeted for training and education. Working as part of a team to train others is the goal of many international service programs that use midwives.

As a midwife who goes overseas, what can you expect? It is important to realize that you must work in co-operation with the government and people in your host country. Don't expect to turn the system of health care upside down. Cultural factors must be taken into account as well. Practicing midwifery abroad is not something to be taken lightly. You'll work hard, sometimes under less-than-pleasant conditions. You may have to pay your own way. You may be faced with poverty, political instability, and language and cultural barriers.

But the rewards can be tremendous. Donna Vidam, a midwife in East Hartford, Connecticut, spent two weeks in Nicaragua, where she delivered two babies and taught workshops for indigenous midwives. One of the babies she delivered was the mother's ninth child; the other was the mother's fourteenth! Vidam participated in the MADRE **Health and Education Skills Exchange**. MADRE is a nonprofit women's organization based in New York that has projects in Nicaragua, El Salvador, Guatemala, the Caribbean, the Middle East, and the U.S. MADRE has "sister relationships" with women's organizations abroad, and together they organize projects for women and their families. Midwives who volunteer for projects raise their own funds; Vidam held a fundraiser for her trip. In her case, the money she raised also helped to pay the food and lodging expenses for the local midwives who participated in the workshops.

"I learned a lot," Vidam says. "I took away at least as much as I gave." Among other things, she learned how to turn a breech baby. To the local midwives, who had less scientific knowledge and technology, things considered "abnormal" in the United States, such as twins and breech births, were considered "no big deal." "I realized that the parameters of normal are very different" from culture to culture, Vidam says.

Vidam found it fascinating to observe cultural differences and local midwifery practices. Midwives from rural areas, who had little in the way of equipment, could even feel the baby's heartbeat just by putting their fingers on the mother's belly. Vidam and an American nurse practitioner held workshops for local midwives in prenatal care, birth, and postpartum care, in addition to sexually transmitted diseases, contraception, and domestic violence. An interpreter helped them to communicate to the midwives in Spanish. "We were treated like royalty," Vidam says. "We met with mayors, with members of the legislature."

The experience was also difficult in some ways. "It was really hard to see the poverty," Vidam says. Because of the political situation in Nicaragua, she adds, MADRE has not sent anyone there as a volunteer since she went, although, of course, the situation is different from country to country.

MADRE
121 West 27th Steet
New York, NY 10001
(212) 627-0444

Project Concern is a nonprofit organization based in San Diego that works with primary health care training and development. It has a service called **Options**, which provides referrals and recruitment for health positions overseas. A sample listing for a nurse-midwife position in the Options newsletter:

"Newly opened nonprofit clinic overlooking Lake Atitlan in Guatemala seeks nurse-midwives to help serve the poor population of the Quiché Maya. Volunteers will work in an outpatient clinic five days a week and assist in the teaching-training of health promoters, traditional birth attendants, and patients. Airfare from Houston, Texas, to Guatemala, food and lodging are provided. Short- and long-term positions are available."

The same Options newsletter listed similar positions in Cambodia, Latvia, the Marshall Islands, Mozambique, Nigeria, and Somalia.

Project Concern International
3550 Afton Road
San Diego, CA 92123
(619) 279-9690

The **International Medical Corps**, based in Los Angeles, was established in 1984 to provide health care and training to areas in crisis throughout the world. Their assignments require a one-year commitment. Transportation, room and board, salary, and insurance are provided. Afghanistan, Pakistan, Bosnia, and Somalia are among the areas served.

International Medical Corps
12233 West Olympic Boulevard
Los Angeles, CA 90064-1052
(310) 826-7800

Project Hope, a project of the People-to-People Health Foundation in Virginia, has paid and volunteer positions for midwives in such areas of the former Soviet Union as Kazhakstan or Ukraine and in other

79

parts of the world. Project Hope is active in the United States, too, with projects for Native Americans and U.S.-Mexican border residents. Applicants must have at least two years of work experience. The work involves "counterpart teaching," both training and learning from host-country colleagues. Salary and round-trip transportation are paid.

The Project Hope Health Sciences Education Center
Millwood, VA 22646
(703) 837-2100

The **Peace Corps** is a program operated by the U.S. government that places volunteers in two-year assignments all over the world. Volunteers with degrees or certification in health fields are needed to work in public health education and to train coworkers in the host country. All expenses are covered, and upon returning home, you receive a "readjustment allowance" (generally about $5,000). The selection process is competitive. You will probably need several years' work experience in addition to your degree or certificate. Midwifery applicants are in demand at the moment.

Peace Corps
1990 K Street NW
Washington, DC 20526
(202) 606-3387

Improving the quality of health care in rural villages that still suffer from the effects of war in El Salvador is the goal of the **International Medical Relief Fund**. Volunteers carry out a community midwife training project. Midwife candidates are chosen from the rural communities and come to a central location for training.

American certified nurse-midwives are needed to direct the program; fluency in Spanish is required.

International Medical Relief Fund
PO Box 1194
Salinas, CA 93902
(408) 758-4001

Another organization that sponsors projects in Central America is the **National Central America Health Rights Network**. To date, the Network has sponsored two CNMs in El Salvador, who have worked with traditional birth attendants.

National Central America Health Rights Network
Eleven Maiden Lane
New York, NY 10038
(212) 732-4790

More information about international health organizations can be obtained from the American College of Nurse-Midwives Special Projects Section, 818 Connecticut Avenue, Washington, DC 20006; (202) 728-9881.

MIDWIFERY AROUND THE WORLD

Even if you decide not to stray from home territory, reading and learning about birth in other cultures can give you invaluable insight as you develop your own unique philosophy of birth. Since midwives deliver 85 percent of babies born all over the world, your colleagues are everywhere. In Europe alone, 75 percent of all births are attended by midwives. In some countries, such as Norway, that percentage is even higher. In indigenous cultures, the folklore of birth is especially rich, and some traditional practices that may seem strange to us

81

are still in use. For example, among the Tonga people of the South Pacific, a woman labors while sitting on her mother's lap on a soft floor. In cases where a baby is not coming out, a Guatemalan midwife may boil a purple onion in beer and have the laboring woman drink the liquid. In Russia, underwater births are much more common than in the United States. Zuñi women of the southwestern United States used to give birth lying on one side, facing the midwife.

It is interesting that in some societies where women are considered to have a lower position than men in the social hierarchy, being a midwife is a way of gaining power and prestige. As a midwife, a woman becomes an important person in the community and may even achieve a degree of economic independence. In Guatemala, for example, midwives enjoy a special status and autonomy.

The status of midwifery in other countries also sheds light on our own policies toward midwives. In Germany, for instance, a 1938 law makes it mandatory for midwives to be present at all births—even births attended by doctors. This is in striking contrast to the American situation, where in some states nurse-midwives must still be supervised by a physician. Perhaps we can learn something from the World Health Organization's recommendation that midwives should be the primary caregivers for normal childbearing women.

The International Confederation of Midwives is an alliance of local, national, and professional organizations of midwives, with the objective of advancing education and knowledge of midwifery and thereby improving the standard of care provided to women and children around the world. Founded in Belgium after World War I, the ICM held international conferences and campaigned for such issues as the right of midwives to adminster pharmacological methods of pain relief. The ICM has created a definition of the midwife that has been ratified by the World Health Organization and the International Federation of Obstetricians and Gynecologists:

A midwife is a person who, having been regularly admitted to a midwifery educational programme, and duly recognized in the country in which it is located, has successfully completed the prescribed course of studies in midwifery and has acquired the requisite qualifications to be registered and/or legally licensed to practice midwifery. She must be able to give the necessary supervision, care and advice to women during pregnancy, labor and the postpartum period, to conduct deliveries on her own responsibility and to care for the newborn and the infant. This care includes preventative measures, the detection of abnormal conditions in mother and child, the procurement of medical assistance and the execution of emergency measures in the absence of medical help. She has an important task in health counselling and education, not only for the women, but also within the family and the community. The work should involve antenatal education and preparation for parenthood and extends to certain areas of gynecology, family planning and child care. She may practice in hospitals, clinics, health units, domiciliary conditions or in any other service.

8

Midwifery-Related Careers

You can make midwifery a part of your life without being a midwife. Your involvement with midwifery can range from teaching childbirth preparation classes one night a week to attending births of friends as a doula to catering to pregnant women in your business. This chapter will introduce you to your many options in the world of midwifery if you are:

- Someone interested in supporting the growth of midwifery
- A prospective midwife looking for experience in the field
- An experienced midwife hoping to branch out from clinical practice
- A person committed to empowering women to improve their health.

CHILDBIRTH ASSISTANTS

A 1991 study showed that the presence of a person providing labor support and educational counseling during childbirth is beneficial to the birthing woman, resulting in shorter labor, improved interaction between parent and baby, and less incidence of cesarean section. The *New England Journal of Medicine* reported: "Women attended by childbirth assistants have shorter labors, use less pain relief medication, and have fewer cesarean sections. They also stroke, smile at, and talk to their newborns more than mothers who have labored alone."

One way that midwives recommend gaining hands-on experience in childbirth is to become a childbirth assistant. A childbirth assistant provides labor support and educational counseling to a woman throughout her childbearing years. Becoming a childbirth assistant can be either a stepping-stone to a midwifery career or a career in itself. Certification with the National Association of Childbirth Assistants qualifies you to set up a professional community-based practice. Among other opportunities available to you as a childbirth assistant are:

- Specializing in working with a particular group in your community, such as pregnant teenagers
- Combining childbirth assisting with another specialty such as massage therapy or hypnotherapy
- Starting your own referral or resource center
- Working with a doctor or midwife.

The **National Association of Childbirth Assistants**, which was founded in 1985, works to establish and strengthen the role of childbirth assistants in maternity care. NACA offers certification for three levels of childbirth assisting. Level I is the basic level; Level II provides advanced training as both a childbirth assistant and a childbirth educator; and Level III offers certification as a perinatal or parent educator. NACA offers other opportunities to educate, as either a Skill Builder Instructor (teaching community workshops) or as a Principal Consultant and Educator (teaching "Becoming a Childbirth Assistant" workshops).

NACA stresses an "empowerment model of care" in

which clients are encouraged to feel confident and self-empowered. The childbirth assistant's program of care consists of:

- two to three prenatal visits
- phone consultation
- being present for labor, birth, and recovery
- two to three postnatal visits
- techniques including communication and counseling, birth plan counseling, postpartum counseling, information, education, support, guidance, and labor coping skills.

NACA's two-day workshops for Level I certification are held in cities around the country. Trained educators can apply to teach workshops in their own communities, so even if you're not in a big city you may still be able to find a workshop near you. The NACA office can help you find the workshop that is most convenient. Certification is granted after the student has completed three study modules after the course, through written correspondence. There are no educational or skill requirements for the workshops. Videos, lectures, discussion, printed materials, and hands-on practice are used to teach the material.

National Association of Childbirth Assistants
205 Copco Lane
San Jose, CA 95123
(800) 868-NACA

Another program for Childbirth Assistant certification is **Informed Birth and Parenting**, Ann Arbor, Michigan. Since 1987, more than 2,200 people have earned certification through Informed Birth and Parenting. Like NACA, Informed Birth and Parenting holds weekend workshops around the country. The workshops cover topics such as assessing fetal heart tones, pelvic exam, and placental exam, as well as instruction in setting up your own business and building a clientele. In addition to the workshop, students seeking certification must complete a required reading list, become certified for infant CPR, write and receive written evaluations of births attended, and complete a written exam. It generally takes about a year to complete all of the requirements and become certified.

Becoming a birth assistant can be a way to supplement your income, as well. Childbirth assistants typically charge clients $150 to $400 per birth.

DOULAS

The idea of a support person at birth is very old, and common in many societies. The word *doula* comes from the Greek, meaning "to be of service to" or "caregiver." In ancient Greek households, the doula was the most important female servant of the house. Today, doulas work with women and their families before and after the baby is born and sometimes provide labor support as well. A doula's role is to provide emotional support throughout the entire labor, assist the woman and her partner in making informed choices and preparing for the birth, and facilitating communication between the woman, her partner, and care providers.

If you aren't sure whether you want to plunge right into midwifery, being a doula is a great way to be involved in the birth process and the setting up of a new family. There is the potential to make important contacts with midwives should you choose to apprentice later on. You can learn a great deal just by observing what goes on during and after the birth, while at the same time being a tremendous help to the family.

In *Mothering the Mother: How a Doula Can Help*

You Have a Shorter, Easier, and Healthier Birth,
Marshall and Phyllis Klaus and John Kennell describe
the qualities of an effective doula: being comfortable
with the sights and sounds of labor, being comfortable
with touching, being tactful and able to get along with
hospital staff, and respecting the parents' independence.
The authors also cite evidence that a doula-assisted birth
can shorten first labor by an average of two hours.

How does one become a doula? There may be a doula
program or organization in your area; check in the
phone book under "childbirth" or "doula." Some
hospitals use doulas and may be able to tell you who
their contacts are. In addition, some midwifery schools,
such as the Seattle Midwifery School, offer doula
training.

Doulas of North America can provide you with more
information about doulas and about training programs
near you. An international organization, DONA is based
in Washington state. Its purpose is to certify doulas
according to an international standard and to serve as
liaison between doulas and the public by encouraging
more people to become doulas and by helping parents to
find doula services.

DONA (Doulas of North America)
1100 23rd Avenue East
Seattle, WA 98112

The arrival of a new baby in a household means a lot
of work and stress for the baby's family. After all,
newborns can be pretty demanding, and if the family
already has other children or if one or both parents are
working, it can be difficult to get everything done. This
is where a postpartum doula becomes involved. A
postpartum doula assists the family after the birth of the
baby. **The National Association of Postpartum Care**

Services offers training for postpartum doulas. Doulas provide valuable help to new parents in this busy time. They can assist with household tasks, child care, support for the new mother, and more, freeing up time for the new parent or parents to rest, spend time with the baby, or do other things.

National Association of Postpartum Care Services, Inc.
326 Shields Street
San Francisco, CA 94132-2734
(415) 587-0219

CHILDBIRTH EDUCATORS

As a childbirth educator, you can help to improve the childbirth experience for parents by providing them with accurate, up-to-date information. With the many alternatives in birth care that are available, parents are faced with many choices. What kind of birth environment do we want? Do we want a doctor or a midwife? How can we have the kind of birth we want in a medically safe way? A childbirth educator is equipped with the knowledge to help parents make wise choices. As choices multiply and parents become more interested in exploring alternatives, the need for qualified childbirth educators will certainly grow.

Childbirth educators are trained in many areas, such as anatomy, nutrition, newborn care, and exercise. They know about the technology used in birth and its advantages and disadvantages. They inform parents about what labor will be like, and what is normal or abnormal. They show mothers techniques for coping during labor, such as relaxation or visualization. They instruct parents about their rights and choices as consumers of childbirth care.

The Certified Perinatal Educators Association provides certification through workshops and training manuals, qualifying you to teach childbirth preparation classes in your community.

Childbirth educators are often trained in one of the established methods of childbirth preparation. The Read method, developed by Grantly Dick-Read, combines relaxation techniques and education of the parents to break what Read believed was a fear-tension-pain cycle. Read believed that if women were more prepared for birth, they would fear it less and would experience less pain as a result.

The Lamaze method, named after the French doctor Fernand Lamaze, also incorporates education and relaxation techniques, but relies on the principle that mothers can be conditioned to view birth in a different way. Lamaze based his idea on the experiments by the Russian doctor Pavlov, which found that dogs could be conditioned to recognize an electric shock as a signal that they would be receiving food rather than as painful. Similarly, Lamaze reasoned, women giving birth could be conditioned to experience the pain of childbirth in a productive way, keeping in mind that they would soon have a beautiful baby. The mother, according to the Lamaze method, should learn useful responses to her pain rather than passive ones.

The Bradley method places emphasis on diet and exercise before birth and deep abdominal breathing during labor. The Bradley method, also known as husband-coached childbirth, advocates nonmedicated births during which a woman works with her body and concentrates on how her body is feeling rather than distracting herself from it.

The following programs offer training and certification as a childbirth educator.

CHILDBIRTH EDUCATION CERTTIFICATION PROGRAMS
Academy of Certified Birth Educators
2001 East Prairie Circle
Olathe, KS 66062
(913) 782-5116
(800) 444-8223

American Academy of Husband-Coached Childbirth
  (Bradley Method)
PO Box 5224
Sherman Oaks, CA 91413-5224
(818) 788-6662/(800) 42-BIRTH

American Society for Psychoprophylaxis in Obstetrics
(ASPO/Lamaze)
1101 Connecticut Avenue
Washington, DC 20036
(800) 368-4404

Birthchoice
17 Stellman Road
Roslindale, MA 02131
(617) 327-3248

Birth Works Cesarean Prevention Movement, Inc.
PO Box 152
Syracuse, NY 13210
(315) 424-1942

Certified Perinatal Educators Association
205 Copco Lane
San Jose, CA 95123
(707) 537-1501

Dallas Association for Parent Education
13551 North Central Expressway
Dallas, TX 75243

Family Life and Maternity Education, Inc.
PO Box 1836
Woodbridge, VA 22193

Gamper International, Inc.
627 Beaver Road
Glenview, IL 60025
(312) 998-6547

Informed Homebirth/Informed Birth and Parenting
PO Box 3675
Ann Arbor, MI 48106
(313) 662-6857

International Childbirth Education Association (ICEA)
PO Box 20048
Minneapolis, MN 55420-0048
(612) 854-8660

National Association of Childbirth Education
  Specialists
8 Sylvan Glen
East Lyme, CT 06333
(914) 962-1781
(800) 822-4256

Positive Pregnancy and Parenting Fitness
51 Saltrock Road
Baltic, CT 06330
(800) 433-5523 (in CT: 822-8573)

Read Natural Childbirth Foundation, Inc.
PO Box 956
San Rafael, CA 94915
(415) 456-8462

The Childbirth Education Association of Metropolitan
   New York, Inc.
PO Box 2036
New York, NY 10185
(212) 757-6300

MASSAGE THERAPY

How might you incorporate massage therapy and childbirth care? In almost all countries of the world, massage
is considered a key component of the care of a pregnant
woman and her new baby. Massage is used during labor
by some midwives as well. As a massage therapist, you
could specialize in services to pregnant women. Massage
has numerous physical and psychological benefits for
everyone, but for pregnant women in particular it can
help to relieve some of the uncomfortable symptoms
such as headaches, cramps, indigestion, and varicose
veins. Massage can also train the body to relax muscles
individually, which is helpful in labor. After completing
a program of study in massage or shiatsu, you need
to be licensed by your state as a Licensed Massage
Therapist (LMT).

EDUCATION

Perhaps you see yourself not as an actively practicing
midwife, but as an educator who will inspire and guide
new students in their midwifery studies. This is certainly
an option if you believe you have the skills to teach well
and if you enjoy an academic environment and lifestyle.
Becoming an educator in midwifery might be something
to shoot for in the future, after you have worked for a
while in a clinical setting. More teaching positions are
available in the field of nurse-midwifery, as many
medical schools have midwifery programs, but if you
have an entrepreneurial spirit, you might consider
starting your own direct-entry education program.

PUBLIC HEALTH

Studying about the origins of disease and health problems and researching the best way to eliminate them is the domain of persons in the field of public health. If you are fascinated by maternal/child health issues and want to contribute to decision-making, rather than being a care provider, public health may be your chance to make a difference. Going back to school for a master's or doctoral degree in public health is an option for midwives who want to apply their experience to the study of public health issues. You can contribute your opinions to the formation of public health policies. You can teach and conduct research at a major university. The possibilities are endless.

9

Planning Your Future

Perhaps you've read all about midwifery and you think it might be something that interests you. "But," you may be wondering, "is it really for me? Do I have what it takes?"

Some midwives report that they simply felt they were meant to become midwives: Ever since they first heard about the field, it was the only thing they wanted to do. Other midwives, after their own birth experiences or previous jobs, simply fell into midwifery, almost by accident. Others make the decision practically, deciding that midwifery offers the best opportunity for them to do what they want to do.

As with any career decision, it is important to evaluate your own skills, talents, strengths, and weaknesses before embarking upon something new. As one midwife says: "The truer sense of yourself you have, the better you will be at birth. You must be a loving person and do everything you can for that woman. It requires great humility—you must always be respectful of the process. It is such an intimate experience. You see someone come through something amazing." "Warm and empathetic" is how another midwife describes a good midwife.

Do you see yourself as a "people person," or do you prefer to work with computers, numbers, or words?

"People skills" are important. You need to develop a trust with your clients; they will need to be honest with you, and they will expect you to be honest with them. You may have to tell them things they do not want to hear. It may be difficult at times to get them to comply with your recommendations on how to take care of themselves and their babies. Good negotiating skills and a good "bedside manner" are crucial. You must be sensitive to the special needs of a client who has experienced sexual or physical abuse, for example, or a client who is reluctant to breast-feed. The extent to which a caregiver is supportive, attentive, helpful, and informative will greatly influence how a laboring woman and her partner perceive their birth experience.

The emotional aspect of midwifery should not be underestimated. As a midwife, you often make strong emotional connections with your clients. "You get to be good friends with clients," says one direct-entry midwife. "A trust develops." You should expect, as a midwife, to have a strong emotional attachment to your work. If you have not given birth yourself, it may be helpful to talk to women who have had children (your own mother or grandmother, for example) and ask them how they feel about their own birth experiences. Books that contain personal stories about childbirth can be an interesting and valuable way to learn about the extremely intense and powerful nature of the process.

Of course, midwifery is not all about being "touchy-feely." You will be providing serious medical care, not just hugs and kisses. Midwifery demands a sincere commitment to women and their health. It is grounded in the belief that women have a right to high-quality medical care as well as the right to choose what kind of care they receive. Volunteering or working at a women's health clinic or an organization such as Planned Parenthood is a useful way to learn about women's health issues. It can also be a place to test your stomach for working in a medical field—can you see yourself working with medical instruments and dealing with life-and-death issues? Are you the type of person who faints at the sight of blood or panics in a hospital? Do you fold under pressure—or become even more productive? One nurse-midwife mentions a good memory as a useful attribute to have as a midwife, since keeping up with all the new studies and techniques raised in medical literature can be demanding. Ina May Gaskin, author of *Spiritual Midwifery* and a forerunner in the movement to resurrect midwifery, recommends taking up a hobby that requres patience, such as knitting or gardening, if you are not already a patient person.

MIDWIFERY IN THE NINETIES

The new technology of the "information superhighway" has made it possible for midwives all over the world to network with each other, sharing ideas and information about everything from new techniques to job opportunities. A new service called MIDWIFE has been set up just for midwives on the World Wide Web (WWW), a service on the network of computer systems called the Internet. There are also two midwifery email lists, one maintained by *Midwifery Today* magazine and one stored on the MIDWIFE WWW service. Information about this service can be obtained by sending an email message to: midwiferequest@csv.warwick.ac.uk. The midwifery information service offered by World Wide Web has the address http:www.csv.warwick.ac.uk: 8000midwifery.html. It is based at the University of Warwick in Great Britain. As the information super-highway continues to expand and more users log on, midwifery resources will probably expand as well.

WHAT ABOUT MEN?

Since ancient times, the natural attendants for women experiencing childbirth were older female relatives who were able to guide the birthing woman because they had their own birth experiences. In traditional societies, this is frequently still the case. In societies where midwives experienced persecution and discrimination, however, the "natural" order of things was changed as male doctors created the field of obstetrics and entered the traditionally female sphere of childbirth. The growing popularity of midwifery is seen by many as a reclaiming of that sphere by women. But does this view necessarily exclude men who have a genuine interest in the process of childbirth and a commitment to empowering women to have positive birth experiences? There are no official barriers to men who want to practice midwifery, but perhaps because the profession has been traditionally practiced by women, few men actually become midwives. (Male midwives are not uncommon in some parts of the world, such as Hawaii.) It is estimated that one percent of all midwives in the United States are men. Men should be aware that many women who seek alternatives to standard hospital childbirth are looking specifically for a "woman-centered" birth environment and may balk at the idea of having a male midwife. However, there are certain to be many women who are open to the idea. As in the field of nursing, perhaps the number of men in the ranks of midwives will grow over time and a male midwife will no longer be an oddity. For the sake of gender equality, it seems reasonable that as women enter fields traditionally dominated by men, men also have the freedom to enter traditionally "female" fields.

"Don't expect to find a male mentor in the field, or guys you can pal around with after work," says Peter Johnson, a midwife with a health maintenance organization (HMO) in Buffalo, New York. "You have to be comfortable having friendships with women." Johnson came to midwifery through nursing, which he studied in the Air Force. While he was enlisted, Johnson says, he had the opportunity to work with many nurses, male and female. When he decided to enter nursing, he had male role models. He was also attracted to nursing because of its flexibility as a career. "I knew it would offer me a wide array of choices," he says.

There is still a stigma attached to a man who enters a career traditionally dominated by women, Johnson says. "We're socialized early on to go into certain careers," he explains. But he has never had a problem being accepted by clients, and he says his role is no different from that of a female midwife. "I didn't go to male midwifery school—I went to midwifery school," he says. "I valued the same things as other nursing students. I wanted to nurture people. I wanted to enter a caring profession. It fit me.

"Midwifery is not the easiest path to take, whether you're a man or a woman," he adds. "But it is a clinically challenging, satisfying career. You get to be with people in a very special time in their lives. I feel very honored to be involved with childbirth."

As advice to prospective midwives, Johnson says, "Midwifery is a profession that is growing and pioneering. I always tell students that they have to take up the torch and they have to fight. They will have to fight barriers in the health care system, and in people's perceptions of midwives. You're constantly fighting. You need to have a dedication that goes beyond 'I want to deliver babies.'"

JOB-HUNTING STRATEGIES

You may graduate from midwifery school with a job lined up at a hospital or birth center. For example, if

99

you received financial aid for midwifery school from a program such as the National Health Service, you may be required to work for a certain period of time in a medically underserved area. If you need to do some serious job-hunting, don't worry. You have an advantage over people in many other professions in that midwifery jobs are plentiful in many parts of the country.

The program from which you graduate should have a placement office with information about job openings. If you are a direct-entry midwife, you can become your own placement office, using word of mouth, advertising in local publications (particularly those geared toward women or people interested in holistic living), or even distributing flyers about your services. A health foods store, for example, might be an appropriate place to find clients who are interested in birth alternatives. "Networking" at midwifery conferences can be another useful way to make job contacts, and advertisements in midwifery- and birth-oriented publications can lead to employment.

10

Midwives and the Health Care Debate

An advertisement for nurse-midwives by a District of Columbia hospital reads: "Help us create the health care system of the future." What the health care system of the future will be is, of course, something that is very much open to debate. Many Americans are fed up with the exorbitant fees charged by doctors and hospitals, but they still want the same quality of care to which they have become accustomed. In this context, midwives are becoming key players in the maze of health care options. As midwives continue to prove themselves, as they have for decades in other countries, perhaps the popularity of medicalized hospital birth will also change. More than obstetricians, midwives can position themselves as primary care providers because they care for women throughout their reproductive lives. The trend in health care today is to consolidate and streamline so that primary care providers can provide more services in a cost-effective way (rather than having patients go to high-priced specialists). Indeed, the success of midwives in hospitals that provide services to low-income patients has already proved that midwives provide high-quality, less expensive care.

An editorial in the San Francisco *Chronicle* (January

1992) stated: "The key to having healthy babies and healthy mothers in California is having competent, relatively inexpensive medical care available before, during and after the birth process." The editorial went on to praise a bill proposed by State Senator Lucy Killea to legalize practice by midwives. It concluded: "This is an idea whose time has very definitely come. It is good for women and good for babies."

Prenatal care is a crucial component of lowering maternal-child health care costs in the United States. When a mother receives care throughout her pregnancy and is taught how to eat, exercise, and care for herself, she has a healthier baby. Complications can be detected and dealt with early on. Women who receive good prenatal care are less likely to have babies prematurely. Seven to ten billion dollars could be saved every year by providing prenatal care to all women. Further, over $8 billion could be saved by putting 75 percent of pregnancies into the hands of midwives. Some states, such as Florida, recognize the money-saving potential of midwifery care. Florida's top health officials have announced a plan to have 50 percent of the state's healthy pregnant women giving birth with midwives by the year 2000. News like this is certainly good for prospective midwives: It seems likely that the need for midwives will only increase as we move into the future.

Glossary

amnesiac   Drug that causes abnormal memory loss.

amniotic   Pertaining to the fluid-filled membrane of the sac enclosing the embryo.

anesthesia   Loss of physical sensation.

apprentice   Person who learns a craft from a skilled worker.

dilate   To expand or swell.

embryo   Living being in its earliest stages of development.

episiotomy   Incision of the perineum, performed during childbirth to prevent injury to the vagina.

fetus   Developing human being in the uterus.

forceps   Hand-held instrument for grasping or pulling objects.

gynecology   Branch of medicine dealing with women's diseases and hygiene.

hallucinogenic   Pertaining to a substance that induces hallucinations.

hormone   Product of living cells that circulates in body fluids and has a specific effect on some other cells.

labor   The physical activities involved in childbirth.

laceration   A rough tear.

malpractice   Failure in professional skill resulting in injury, loss, or damage.

massage   Rubbing and kneading of the body for therapeutic effect.

menopause   The natural cessation of menstrual periods.

misogynistic   Pertaining to hatred of women.

obstetrician   Practitioner of the branch of medicine dealing with childbirth.

Pap smear Test to sample cervical secretions, used for the detection of cancer and other abnormal conditions.

perineum The small area between the anus and the vulva in the female.

placenta The organ that joins the fetus to the uterus and nourishes the fetus.

postpartum After birth.

prenatal Before birth.

protocol Code of procedure or etiquette.

reimburse To pay back.

sterile Free from germs.

uterus The muscular organ in a female mammal in which the young develop before birth.

Appendix

FOR MORE INFORMATION
The American College of Nurse-Midwives
1522 K Street NW
Washington, DC 20005
(202) 728-9860

American Foundation for Maternal and Child Health
30 Beekman Place
New York, NY 10022
(212) 759-5510

Birth and Bonding Family Center
1172 San Pablo Avenue
Berkeley, CA 94702
(510) 527-2121

The Boston Women's Health Book Collective
240A Elm Street
Somerville, MA 02144
(617) 625-0271

The Farm Midwifery Center
48 The Farm
Summertown, TN 38483
(615) 964-2293

Frontier School of Midwifery and Family Nursing
PO Box 528
Hyden, KY 41749
(606) 672-2312

Informed Homebirth/Informed Birth and Parenting
PO Box 3675
Ann Arbor, MI 48106
(313) 662-6857

International Association of Parents and Professionals
  for Safe Alternatives in Childbirth (NAPSAC)
Route 1, Box 646
Marble Hill, MO 63764
(314) 238-2010

International Childbirth Education Association
PO Box 20048
Minneapolis, MN 55240
(612) 854-8660

International Cesarean Awareness Network, Inc.
PO Box 152
Syracuse, NY 13210
(315) 424-1942

La Leche League International, Inc.
9616 Minneapolis Avenue
Franklin Park, IL 60631
(708) 455-7730

Midwifery Communication and Accountability Project
  (MCAP)
15 Saxon Terrace
Newton, MA 02161
(617) 630-8044

Midwifery Today and Childbirth Education
PO Box 2672
Eugene, OR 97402
1-800-743-0974/(503) 344-7438

Midwives Alliance of North America
PO Box 175
Newton, KS 67114
(316) 283-4543

National Association of Childbearing Centers
3123 Gottschall Road
Perkiomenville, PA 18074
(215) 234-8068

National Black Women's Health Project
1615 M Street NW
Washington, DC: 20036
(202) 835-0117

National Center for Education in Maternal and Child
   Health
2000 15th Street North
Arlington, VA 22201-2617
(703) 524-7802

National College of Naturopathic Medicine
11231 SE Market Street
Portland, OR 97216
(503) 255-4860

National Women's Health Network
1325 G Street NW
Washington, DC 20005
(202) 347-1140

North American Registry of Midwives
PO Box 15
Linn, WV 26384

Pennypress, Inc.
1100 23rd Avenue East
Seattle, WA 98112
(206) 325-1419

Planned Parenthood
810 Seventh Avenue
New York, NY 10019
(212) 541-7800

Waterbirth International
PO Box 366
West Linn, OR 97068
(503) 638-2930

Women's Institute for Childbearing Policy
Box 72
Roxbury, VT 05669
(802) 485-8428

STATE MIDWIFERY ASSOCIATIONS

Midwives Association of Alaska
c/o Shirley Davis
14870 Snowshoe Lane
Anchorage, AK 99516

Arizona Association of Midwives
c/o Lynn Richards
3455 Moki
Sodona, AZ 86336

Arkansas Association of Midwives
c/o Ida Darragh
4322 Country Club
Little Rock, AR 72207

California Association of Midwives
PO Box 417854
Sacramento, CA 95841

Colorado Midwives Association
PO Box 1067
Boulder, CO 80306

Alliance of Connecticut Midwives
61 High Street
Terryville, CT 06786

Chesapeake Midwifery Guild (Washington, DC, and
    Maryland)
8411 48th Avenue
College Park, MD 21207

Midwives' Association of Florida
c/o Karin Kearns
702 W. Adalee Street
Tampa, FL 33603

Florida Friends of Midwives
c/o Becky Martin
1810 28th Street W.
Bradenton, FL 34205

Georgia Midwives Association
PO Box 29633
Atlanta, GA 30359

Idaho Midwifery Council
c/o Kathleen McDonald
2115 North 29th Street
Boise, ID 83703-5847

Illinois Alliance of Midwives
c/o Yvonne Cryns
PO Box 1472
Arlington Heights, IL 60006

Indiana Midwives Association
c/o Linda Morgan
10017 East 1000 Street
Upland, IN 46989

Mid-America Midwives' Alliance
28 Forest Hill Place NE
Iowa City, IA 52240

Kansas Midwives Association
c/o Kelly Brace
10002 East Lincoln Street
Wichita, KS 67202

Midwives of Maine
c/o Jill Breen
RFD 1
St. Albans, ME 04971

Massachusetts Friends of Midwives
PO Box 3188
Boston, MA 02130

Massachusetts Midwives' Alliance
PO Box 112
Fiskdale, MA 01518

Michigan Midwives' Association
Rte. 1 Loop Road
Hesperia, MI 48421

Minnesota Midwives Guild
PO Box 57
Hendrum, MN 56550

Montana Midwives' News
PO Box 3302
Missoula, MT 59806

Nebraska Midwives' Association
c/o Karen Gourley
9508 Burdette Circle
Omaha, NE 68134

Nevada Midwives' Alliance
5770 Pioneer Avenue
Las Vegas, NV 89102

New Mexico Association of Midwives
PO Box 40647
Albuquerque, NM 87196

Midwives' Alliance of New York
PO Box 1000
Warwick, NY 10990

Carolina Association for the Advancement of Midwifery
Rte. 1, Box 210M
Durham, NC 27705

North Dakota Midwives' Alliance
PO Box 1074
Casselton, ND 58012-1074

Ohio Midwives Alliance
1085 Country Road 601, RR2
Ashland, OH 44805

Oregon Midwifery Council
5705 NE Duniway Street
Dayton, OR 97114

Pennsylvania Midwives' Association
RD 3 Box 41A
Spartansburg, PA 16434

Tennessee Midwives Association
116 Clifton Court
Old Hickory, TN 37138
(615) 847-0774

Association of Texas Midwives
603 West 13th Street
Austin, TX 78701

Vermont Midwives' Alliance
c/o Judy Luce
30 Park Street
Barre, VT 05641

Commonwealth Midwives' Alliance (Virginia)
RT 2, Box 607
Amissville, VA 22002

Midwives' Association of Washington State
2524 16th Ave. South
Seattle, WA 98144

or: 415 38th Street NE
Olympia, WA 98506

Midwives' Alliance of West Virginia
PO Box 28
Greenwood, WV 26360

Wisconsin Guild of Midwives
c/o Ginnie Felch
Rte. 1, Box 227
Cascade, WI 53011

Alliance of Wisconsin Midwives
Trout Creek Road, Box 210
Soldier Grove, WI 54655

Midwives' Alliance of Wyoming
PO Box 5131
Cheyenne, WY 82003

DIRECT-ENTRY EDUCATION PROGRAMS

Academy of Midwifery Arts
330 "A" Untah
Colorado Springs, CO 80903

Apprentice Academics
The Midwifery Home Study Course
PO Box 788
Claremore, OK 74018-0788
(918) 342-1335

Austin Area Birthing Center
8500 North Mopac Street
Austin, TX 78759
(512) 346-3224 ·

Bastyr College
144 NE 54th Street
Seattle, WA 98105
(206) 523-9585 ·

Birthingway Midwifery School
5731 North Williams Street
Portland, OR 97217
(503) 283-4996.

Connecticut Friends of Midwives
54 Fairview Drive
Madison, CT 06443

Family Birth Services
814 Dalworth Street
Grand Prairie, TX 75050

Fellowship of Christian Midwives and Childbirth
  Educators International
PO Box 642
Parker, CO 80134
(303) 841-2128

Florida School of Traditional Midwifery
4220 NW 20th Street
Gainesville, FL 32609
(904) 338-0766

Frazier Valley School of Midwifery
c/o MTF Box 65343
Sta S
Vancouver, BCV5N 5P3
Canada

Holistic Midwifery Training
PO Box 204
Barringon, RI 02806

Hygieia College
Box 398
Monroe, UT 84754
(801) 527-3738 or (801) 527-3219

Massachusetts Midwives' Alliance Study Course
368 Village Street
Millis, MA 02054

Maternidad La Luz
1308 Magoffin Street
El Paso, TX 79901
(915) 532-5895 ·

National School of Technology
16150 NE 17th Avenue N.
Miami Beach, FL 33162
(305) 949-9500·

New Life Birth Services
2311 West 9th Street
Austin, TX 78703
(512) 477-5452

Northern Arizona Institute of Midwifery
PO Box 1929
Flagstaff, AZ 86002
(602) 779-6064

North New Mexico Midwifery and National College of
  Midwifery
Drawer CS
Taos, NM 87571

Oregon School of Midwifery
PO Box 23331
Eugene, OR 97402
(503) 689-0464
Tow-year certificate program

Sage Femme Midwife School
PO Box 2014
Clackamas, OR 97015

Seattle Midwifery School
2524 16th Avenue S
Seattle, WA 98144 ·
(206) 322-8834

The Traditional Childbearing Group
136 Warren Street
Roxbury, MA

Utah School of Midwifery
Diane Bjarnson
PO Box 793
Pleasant Grove, UT 84062

CERTIFICATE PROGRAMS
Baylor College of Medicine
Dept. of OB/GYN
Smith Towers
6550 Fannin
Houston, TX 77030
(713) 793-3541, 3542

Baystate Medical Center
Nurse-Midwifery Education Progam
689 Chestnut Street
Springfield, MA 01199
(413) 784-4448

Charles R. Drew University of Medicine and Science
Nurse-Midwifery Education Program
College of Allied Health Sciences
1621 East 120th Street
Los Angeles, CA 90059
(213) 563-4951, 603-4611

Community-Based Nurse-Midwifery Education
   Program
Frontier School of Midwifery and Family Nursing
PO Box 528
Hyden, KY 41749

Education Program Associates
Midwifery Education Program
1 West Campbell Avenue
Campbell, CA 95008
(408) 374-3720

Parkland School of Nurse-Midwifery
Parkland Memorial Hospital
SW Medical Center at Dallas
5th Flr., WCS Dept.
5201 Harry Hines Boulevard
Dallas, TX 75235
(214) 590-8597 or 8107

117

State University of New York
Health Science Center at Brooklyn
Nurse-Midwifery Program
Box 1227, 450 Clarkson Avenue
Brooklyn, NY 11203
(718) 270-7740 or 7741

University of Medicine and Dentistry of New Jersey
Nurse-Midwifery Program
65 Bergen street
Newark, NJ 07107-3001
(201) 982-4249, 4298

UCSF/SFGH
Interdepartmental Nurse-Midwifery Education Program
SFGH, Ward 6D
1001 Potrero Avenue
San Francisco, CA 94110
(415) 206-5106

University of Southern California
Nurse-Midwifery Educational Program
Women's Hospital
1240 North Mission Road.
Los Angeles, CA 90033

MASTER'S PROGRAMS
Boston University
School of Public Health
MPH/CNM Program
80 East Concord Steet
Boston, MA 02118
(617) 638-5042

Case Western Reserve University
School of Nursing
Nurse-Midwifery Program
10900 Euclid Avenue
Cleveland, OH 44106-4904
(216) 368-3532

Columbia University
Graduate Program in Nurse-Midwifery
School of Nursing
617 West 168th Street
New York, NY 10032
(212) 305-5756

East Carolina University
Nurse-Midwifery Program
School of Nursing
Greenville, NC 27858
(919) 757-6057

Emory University
School of Nursing
Atlanta, GA 30322
(404) 727-6918

Georgetown University
School of Nursing
Graduate Program in Nurse-Midwifery
3700 Reservoir Road NW
Washington, DC 20007
(202) 687-4772

Medical University of South Carolina
Nurse-Midwifery Program
College of Nursing
171 Ashley Avenue
Charleston, SC 29425
(803) 792-3077

Oregon Health Sciences University
School of Nursing
Dept. of Family Nursing
Nurse-Midwifery Program
3181 SW Sam Jackson Park Road
Portland, OR 97201
(503) 494-3822

University of Alabama School of Nursing
Graduate Programs
Nurse-Midwifery Option
University of Alabama at Birmingham
UAB Station
Birmingham, AL 35294-1210

Interdepartmental Nurse-Midwifery Education Program
UCSF School of Nursing
N411X, Box 0606
San Francisco, CA 94143-0606
(415) 476-4694

UCSF/UCSD
Intercampus Graduate Studies
Dept. of Community and Family Medicine, 0809
UCSD School of Medicine
University of California, San Diego
9500 Gilman Drive
La Jolla, CA 92093-0809
(619) 543-5480

University of Colorado
Health Sciences Center
School of Nursing, Graduate Program
Nurse-Midwifery Program
4200 East 9th Avenue
Denver, CO 80262
(303) 270-8654

University of Florida
Health Sciences Center, Jacksonville
Nurse-Midwifery Program
College of Nursing
653 West 8th Street Bldg 1
Jacksonville, FL 32209-6561
(904) 549-3245

University of Illinois at Chicago
College of Nursing
760 Rose Street
Lexington, KY 40536-0232
(606) 233-6650

University of Miami
School of Nursing
D2-5, Royce Building
PO Box 016960
1755 NW 12th Avenue
Miami, FL 33136
(305) 548-4636, 4640

University of Michigan
Nurse-Midwifery Program
School of Nursing
400 North Ingalls Street
Ann Arbor, MI 48109
(313) 763-3710

University of Minnesota
School of Nursing, 6-101 Unit F
308 Harvard Street SE
Minneapolis, MN 55455
(612) 624-6494

University of New Mexico
College of Nursing
Nurse-Midwifery Program
Albuquerque, NM 87131
(505) 277-1184

University of Pennsylvania
School of Nursing
Nursing Education Building
420 Guardian Street
Philadelphia, PA 19104-6096
(215) 898-4335

University of Rhode Island
College of Nursing
White Hall
Kingston, RI 02881-0814
(401)792-2766

University of Texas at El Paso/Texas Tech University
Collaborative Nurse-Midwifery Program
Texas Tech University HSC
Dept. of OB/GYN
4800 Alberta Avenue
El Paso, TX 79905
(915) 545-6490

University of Utah
College of Nursing
Graduate Program in Nurse-Midwifery
25 South Medical Drive
Salt Lake City, UT 84112
(801) 581-8274

Yale University
School of Nursing
Nurse-Midwifery Program
25 Park Street
PO Box 9740
New Haven, CT 06536-0740
(203) 737-2344

PRE-CERTIFICATION PROGRAMS
Jackson Memorial Hospital
University of Miami Medical Center
Nurse-Midwifery Program
Women's Hospital Center
East Tower, 3003
1611 NW 12th Avenue
Miami, FL 33136
(305) 585-6628

STATE HEALTH DEPARTMENTS
(Contact your state health department if you have a
question about midwifery licensing requirements in
your state.)

Alabama Department of Public Health
434 Monroe Street
Montgomery, AL 36130-1701
(205) 242-5095

Alaska Department of Health and Social Services
Pouch H-06
Juneau, AK 99811-0610
(907) 465-3030

Arizona Department of Health Services
1740 West Adams Street
Phoenix, AZ 85007
(602) 542-1024

Arkansas Department of Health
State Health Building
4815 West Markham Street
Little Rock, AR 72205-3867
(501) 661-2112

California Department of Health Services
714 P Street
Sacramento, CA 95814
(916) 445-1248

Colorado Department of Health
4210 East 11th Avenue
Denver, CO 80220
(303) 331-4602

Connecticut Department of Health services
150 Washington Street
Hartford, CT 06106
(203) 566-2038

Delaware Division of Public Health
Department of Health and Social Services
PO Box 637
Dover, DE 19901
(302) 736-4701

District of Columbia Department of Human Services
Commission of Public Health
1660 L Street NW
Washington, DC 20036
(202) 673-7700

Florida Health Program Office
Deaprtment of Health and Rehabilitative Srevices
Building I
1323 Winewood Boulevard
Tallahassee, FL 32399-0700
(904) 488-4115

Georgia Division of Public Health
878 Peachtree Street NE
Atlanta, GA 30309
(404) 894-7505

Hawaii Department of Health
PO Box 3378
Honolulu, HI 96801
(808) 548-6505

Idaho Bureau of Preventive Medicine
Division of Health
Department of Health and Welfare
Towers Building
450 W. State Street
Boise, ID 83720
(208) 334-5930

Illinois Department of Public Health
545 W. Jefferson Street
Springfield, IL 62761
(217) 782-4977

Indiana State Board of Health
PO Box 1964
Indianapolis, IN 46206-1964
(317) 633-8400

Iowa Department of Public Health
Lucas State Office Building
East 12th and Walnut Streets
Des Moines, IA 50319
(515) 281-5605

Kansas Division of Health
Department of Health and Environment
Building 740
Forves Field
Topeka, KS 66620
(913) 296-1500

Kentucky Department for Health Services
Cabinet for Human Resources
Health Services Building
275 East Main Street
Frankfort, KY 40621
(502) 564-3970

Louisiana Department of Hospitals DHH
Office of Public Health Services
PO Box 60630
New Orleans, LA 70160
(504) 568-5052

Maine Bureau of Health
Department of Human Services
State House, Station 11
Augusta, ME 04333
(207) 789-3201

Maryland Department of Health and Mental Hygiene
Herbert R. O'Conor State Office Building
201 West Preston Street
Baltimore, MD 21201
(301) 225-6500

Massachusetts Department of Public Health
150 Tremont Street
Boston, MA 02111
(617) 727-0201

Michigan Department of Public Health
PO Box 30195
Lansing, MI 48909
(517) 335-8000

Minnesota Department of Health
PO Box 9441
Mineapolis, MN 55440
(612) 623-5460

Mississippi Department of Health
PO Box 1700
Jackson, MS 39215-1700
(601) 960-7400

Missouri Department of Health
PO Box 570
Jefferson City, MO 65102
(314) 751-6001

Montana Department of Health and Environmental
 Services
Cogswell Building
Helena, MT 59620
(406) 444-2544

Nebraska Department of Health
PO Box 95007
Lincoln, NE 68509
(402) 471-2133

Nevada Health Division
Capitol Complex
Carson City, NV 89710
(702) 885-4740

New Hampshire Division of Public Health Services
Health and Welfare Services Building
6 Hazen Drive
Concord, NH 03301-6527
(603) 271-4501

New Jersey Department of Health
CN 360
Trenton, NJ 08625
(609) 292-7837

New Mexico Division of Public Health
Harold Runnels Building
1190 St. Francis Drive
Santa Fe, NM 87503
(505) 827-0020

New York Department of Health
Corning Tower
Empire State Plaza
Albany, NY 12237
(518) 474-2011

North Carolina Department of Environment, Health
    and Natural Resources
PO Box 27687
Raleigh, NC 27611
(919) 733-3446

North Dakota Department of Health
State Capitol
600 East Boulevard Avenue
Bismarck, ND 58505-0200
(701) 224-2372

Ohio Department of Health
246 North High Street
Columbus, OH 43226-0588
(614) 466-3543

Oklahoma Department of Health
PO Box 53551
Oklahoma City, OK 73152
(405) 271-4200

Oregon Health Division
PO Box 231
Portland, OR 97207
(503) 229-5032

Pennsylvania Department of Health
PO Box 90
Harrisburg PA 17108
(717) 787-6436

Rhode Island Department of Health
Cannon Building
Three Capitol Hill
Providence, RI 02908
(401) 277-2231

South Crolina Department of Health and
Environmental Control
2600 Bull Street
Columbia, SC 29201
(803) 734-4880

South Dakota Department of Health
Joe Foss Building
523 East Capitol Avenue
Pierre, SD 57501
(605) 773-3361

Tenessee Department of Health and Environment
Cordell Hull Building
Nashville, TN 37219
(615) 741-3111

Texas Department of Health
1100 West 49th Street
Austin, TX 78756-3199
(512) 458-7375

Utah Department of Health
288 North 1460 West Street
Salt Lake City, UT 84116-0700
(801) 538-6101

Vermont Department of Health
PO Box 70
Burlington, VT 05402
(802) 863-7280

Virginia Department of Health
James Madison Building
109 Governor Street
Richmond, VA 23219
(804) 786-3561

Washington Division of Health
Department of Health
Mail Stop ET-21
Olympia, WA 98504
(206) 753-5871

West Virginia Department of Health
State Office Building 3
1800 Washington Street E.
Charleston, WV 25305
(304) 348-2971

Wisconsin Division of Health
PO Box 309
Madison, WI 53701-0309
(608) 266-7568

Wyoming Department of Health and Social Services
Hathaway Building
2300 Capitol Avenue
Cheyenne, WY 82002-0710
(307) 777-7656

For Further Reading

Arms, Suzanne. *Immaculate Deception: A New Look at Women and Childbirth in America*. New York: Bantam, 1986.

Boston Women's Health Book Collective. *The New Our Bodies, Ourselves*. New York: Simon & Schuster, 1992.

Brennan, Barbara. *The Complete Book of Midwifery*. New York: Dutton, 1977.

Courter, Gay. *The Midwife*. Boston: Houghton Mifflin, 1981.

Davis, Elizabeth. *Heart and Hands: A Midwife's Guide to Pregnancy and Birth*. Berkeley: Celestial Arts, 1987.

Edwards, Margot, and Mary Waldorf. *Reclaiming Birth: History and Heroines of American Childbirth Reform*. Trumansburg, NY: Crossing Press, 1984.

Floyd, Robbie Davis. *Birth as an American Right of Passage*. Berkeley: University of California Press, 1992.

Gaskin, Ina May. *Spiritual Midwifery*. Summertown, TN: The Book Publishing Co., 1990.

Kitzinger, Sheila. *The Complete Book of Pregnancy and Childbirth*. New York: Alfred A. Knopf, 1980.

McCartney, Marion, and Antonia van der Meer. *The Midwife's Pregnancy and Childbirth Book*. New York: Henry Holt, 1990.

Mitford, Jessica. *The American Way of Birth*. New York: E.P. Dutton, 1992.

Nilssen, Lennart. *A Child Is Born*, rev.ed. New York: Delacorte Press, 1990.

Rothman, Barbara Katz. *In Labor: Women and Power in the Birthplace*. New York: W. W. Norton, 1992.
Singingtree, Daphne. *Birthsong Midwifery Workbook*. Eugene, OR: Eagle Tree Press, 1993.
Steiger, Carolyn. *Becoming a Midwife*. Portland, OR: Hoogin House, 1987.
Ulrich, Laurel Thatcher. *A Midwife's Tale: The Life of Martha Ballard, Based on Her Diary, 1785–1812*. New York: Vintage, 1990.
Varney, Helen. *Nurse-Midwifery*. Boston: Blackwell Scientific Publications, 1987.

PERIODICALS OF INTEREST
Birth: Issues in Perinatal Care
Blackwell Scientific Publications, Inc.
Journal Fulfillment
238 Main St.
Cambridge, MA 02142
(617) 225-0401

Birth Gazette
42 The Farm
Summertown, TN 38483
(615) 964-2519

Childbirth Instructor
26 Broadway, Suite 733
New York, NY 10004

The Compleat Mother
Box 209
Minot, ND 58702
(701) 852-2822

The Doula
PO Box 71
Santa Cruz, CA 95063-9488

The Journal of Nurse-Midwifery
Elsevier Publishing
655 Avenue of the Americas
New York, NY 10010-5107

Midwifery Today
PO Box 2672
Eugene, OR 97402
(800) 743-0974

Mothering
PO Box 1690
Santa Fe, NM 87504

Index

A
Abrams, Lauren, 30–32, 75
accreditation, 60
activism, political, 54–55
American College of Nurse-
    Midwives (ACNM), 28, 33,
    34, 39
analgesic, 21
anesthesia, 5, 35
    epidural, 21
amniotic fluid, 17
apprenticeship, independent
    midwife, 39–41
autonomous midwifery practice,
    65–66

B
birth center, 11, 26–27, 44, 48,
    58–64, 72–74
birthing stool/chair, 19
birthing suites, hospital, 11, 48
birth settings, 48–69
births, low-risk, 14, 20, 52, 56, 69
Bradley method, 90
breast-feeding, 35
Breckinridge, Mary, 27, 52
breech birth, 20–21
Burkhardt, Patricia, 20, 29

C
certification, 37, 38, 41, 53
certified nurse-midwives, 26–35,
    53, 71–72
    and homebirth, 53–56
cesarean section, 23–24, 30
Childbearing Center, 60–63
childbirth
    classes, 61

husband-coached, 90
    issues of, 13–25
childbirth assistant, 84–85
childbirth educator, 27, 56, 66,
    89–90, 93
Childbirth Services, 65–66
counseling, 32, 35, 55, 85

D
Dick-Read, Grantly, 9, 90
direct-entry midwives, *see*
    independent midwives
doctors
    backup, 55, 60
    gaining influence, 5–6, 9
doula, 87–88
Doulas of North America, 88
drugs, 13, 19, 21

E
education
    certified nurse-midwife, 27–28,
        33–35
    independent midwives, 41–44
electronic fetal monitor, 23, 24–25
embryo, 14–15
episiotomy, 9, 18, 20, 33, 35
experience, hands-on, 34, 39, 42,
    44–45, 53

F
fetus, 15
Fields, Sandra, 53–54
financial aid, 36
forceps, 9, 21
Frontier Nursing Service, 27, 52

G
granny-midwives, 11
gynecological care, 35

H
health maintenance organization, 26, 98, 99
heartbeat, fetal, 17, 24, 39, 78
homebirth, 26, 39, 48, 49–58
hospital
    childbirth in, 6, 65–66, 67–69
    charges for childbirth, 19
    delivery horror stories, 10
    midwifery in, 28–29, 33, 53, 55
Hutchinson, Anne, 4

I
independent midwives, 32, 35, 37–47, 53
    and homebirth, 56–58
    states licensed in, 37–39
Indian Health Service, 74–75
infant mortality, 7–8, 70, 72
Informed Birth and Parenting, 86–87
International Confederation of Midwives, 82–83
International Medical Corps, 79
International Medical Relief Fund, 80–81
Internet, midwifery on the, 97
invasive procedures, 19–25, 68

J
job-hunting, 99–100
Johnson, Peter, 98–99

L
labor, 17–18, 35, 59
Lamaze, Fernand, 9, 90
Lange, Julia, 56–58
Lang, Raven, 11
legislation, homebirth, 52–53
licensure, 28, 35, 37–38, 41, 42, 46, 53, 60

M
MADRE Health and Educational Skills Exchange, 77–78
massage therapy, 85, 93
Maternidad La Luz, 43–44
Maternity Center Association, 60
Medicaid, 32–33, 38, 67, 71
men, as midwives, 5, 98–99
midwifery, history of, 1–12
Midwives' Alliance of North America, 39–40
Montagu, Ashley, 10

N
National Association of Childbearing Centers, 60
National Association of Childbirth Assistants, 85–86
National Association of Postpartum Care Services, 88–89
National Central America Health Rights, 81
National Health Service, 75, 100
natural childbirth, 9–11, 19
Nurse Midwifery Birthing Services (NMBS), 63–65
nutrition, 55, 70, 89

O
obstetrics, as medical specialty, 5, 7, 19
Our Bodies, Ourselves, 10–11
overseas practice, 76–83
oxytocin, 17, 22

P
partnership, independent midwives, 67
Peace Corps, 80
people skills, 96
pitocin, 22
politics, childbirth, 19–25
positions, labor, 18–19, 22–23, 24
postpartum care, 35, 59, 78
pregnancy, 14–17

teenage, 45, 70, 85
prenatal care, 16–17, 27, 30, 32, 35, 59, 61, 65, 70, 74, 78
private practive, 26–27, 55–56, 64–67
Project Concern, 78–79
Project Hope, 79–80
public health, 94
public hospitals, 70–74

R
registered nurse, 33, 55
reimbursement, insurance, 32–33, 46, 52

S
salaries
    certified nurse-midwives, 36, 69
    independent midwife, 45–46
Schwarzchild, Miriam, 54–46
Sellars, Barbara, 61
Sinquefield, Gail, 60–62
support, labor, 69, 72, 85

by certified nurse-midwife, 30, 35
by independent midwife, 39
surgical intervention, 13, 20

T
technology, high, 13, 20, 33, 68, 89
Twilight Sleep (scopalomine), 22

U
Ulrich, Laurel Thatcher, 4–5

V
Vidam, Donna, 77–78

W
waterbirth, 48
well-woman care, 5, 65, 66
Whitney, Lynn, 62–63
Williams, J. Whitridge, 6–7
Wrigley, Rebecca, 44–45